Christian Citizenship

"Terry Webb makes the essential point: Whenever Christians seek to exercise dominion over society, they have abandoned the way of Jesus. This message is the antidote to Christian nationalism."

—**Greg Carey**, Provost, Moravian Seminary, Lancaster Campus

"The book is rich with stories, illustrations, and quotations that help the reader understand the complications in the history of the church and could serve as a textbook for an introduction to church history or supplement a New Testament survey course. It is also suitable for adult Sunday School and other study settings. The author's aim is not just to present facts, but to help followers of Jesus use them to address current challenges facing Christians."

—**Dr. Alex Awad**, Founder, Shepherd's Society

"This challenging book presents one vision of Christian citizenship grounded in the Scriptures and history of the Christian church including its creeds, while criticizing the recent redefinition of Christian identity based on an often judgmental and false view of Christian theology. The exegesis of Jesus' parables provides an excellent basis for the core of a lived and vibrant faith though some may disagree with the author's conclusions about their application."

—**Abigail Rian Evans**, Senior Scholar, Pellegrino Center for Clinical Bioethics, Georgetown University Medical Center

"Both evocative and provocative, *Christian Citizenship* makes a strong case for how Christians are called to live in the world. It also provides a timely and urgent warning of the dangers of Christian nationalism, while insightfully tying that movement to historical examples of the enmeshing of church and state."

—**Adam Russell Taylor**, President, Sojourners

"Mary Theresa Webb offers a sweeping and accessible journey through Christian history that illuminates how religious nationalism has repeatedly distorted the heart of the Gospel. With clarity and pastoral wisdom, she equips readers to recognize the dangers of church-state entanglement in our own time and to reclaim a faith rooted in the Beatitudes. A timely and readable guide for Christians seeking to resist distortion and live with courage and hope."

—**Jen Butler**, Founding CEO, Faith in Democracy

"Webb's winsome introduction to Christian citizenship combines colorful images and bite-sized chapters. Webb is uncompromising in her call to Christians to return to the Christ who said, 'my kingdom is not of this world.' But her book—which ends with a practical guide to dialogue—is, at root, an invitation to a conversation, from one Christian to another."

—**David Ney**, Associate Professor of Church History, Trinity Anglican Seminary

Christian Citizenship

Endangered in America

Mary Theresa Webb

Foreword by Rob Schenck

WIPF & STOCK · Eugene, Oregon

CHRISTIAN CITIZENSHIP
Endangered in America

Wipf & Stock
An Imprint of Wipf and Stock Publishers
199 W. 8th Ave., Suite 3
Eugene, OR 97401

www.wipfandstock.com

PAPERBACK ISBN: 979-8-3852-7020-0
HARDCOVER ISBN: 979-8-3852-7021-7
EBOOK ISBN: 979-8-3852-7022-4

VERSION NUMBER 03/23/26

PERMISSIONS

Scripture quotations marked ERV are taken from the Holy Bible: Easy-to-Read Version (ERV), International Edition © 2013, 2016 by Bible League International. Used by permission.

Scripture quotations marked GNT are taken from the Good News Translation in Today's English Version – Second Edition Copyright © 1992 by American Bible Society. Used by Permission.

Scriptures marked NLT are taken from the Holy Bible, New Living Translation (NLT). Copyright ©1996, 2004, 2007 by Tyndale House Foundation. Used by permission of Tyndale House Publishers, Inc.

Scriptures marked NIV are taken from the Holy Bible, New International Version (NIV). Copyright © 1973, 1978, 1984, 2011 by Biblica, Inc.™ Used by permission. All rights reserved.

Scriptures marked NRSVA are taken from the New Revised Standard Version Bible: Anglicized Edition, copyright © 1989, 1995 the Division of Christian Education of the National Council of the Churches of Christ in the United States of America. Used by permission. All rights reserved.

Scriptures marked MSG are taken from THE MESSAGE. Copyright © by Eugene H. Peterson, 1993, 1994, 1995, 1996, 2000, 2002. Used by permission of NavPress Publishing Group.

Scriptures marked NET are taken from the New English Translation (NET Bible). Copyright ©1996–2006 by Biblical Studies Press, L.L.C. Used by permission. All rights reserved.

Scriptures marked ASV are taken from the American Standard Version (ASV). Public domain.

Scriptures marked CEB are taken from the COMMON ENGLISH BIBLE. Copyright © 2011. All rights reserved. Used by permission.

Scriptures marked RSV are taken from the Revised Standard Version of the Bible, copyright © 1946, 1952, and 1971 the Division of Christian Education of the National Council of the Churches of Christ in the United States of America. Used by permission. All rights reserved.

In remembrance of Tony Campolo and Charles Williams
Prophets of Peace and Justice

Contents

Foreword

In my former role as an activist on the Christian right in Washington, DC, I saw firsthand the power of religiously motivated and informed political activism. I also observed the deleterious effects that political ideologies, co-optation, and overly close alliances between church and state can produce. When religion is placed at the service of politics, it corrupts both sides—the sacred and the secular. That's why I left the national movement I helped lead for over thirty years and became a loving critic of my own highly politicized American evangelical tribe. It's also what eventually connected me to the excellent work of Mary Theresa Webb. In this volume, Dr. Webb offers an insightful analysis and theological examination of Christian nationalism. In doing so, she also provides a solution to this escalating crisis, as such religiopolitical phenomena demand a religious response.

Too often, secular arguments and nonreligious shaming are used in an attempt to convince Christian nationalists that they are wrong and should abandon their mission to transform society into one that reflects their opinions. As history has proven, such approaches are useless. Unless a true believer experiences an epiphany, opening their heart and mind to the cultic error that is Christian nationalism, they will only double down in their resolve to defy their critics by even more passionately espousing and practicing heresy. This is what makes Dr. Webb's *Christian Citizenship: Endangered in America* so timely and uniquely helpful.

Faith-driven followers of religious fallacies must be challenged with faith-driven spiritual truths.

Dr. Webb knows her subject all too well. She is a passionate Christian believer herself. She also has personal and academic knowledge of the evangelical world. As she explains in her preface, "First, I need to confess that I am a born-again believer and follower of Jesus whose spirituality has been enriched through my participation in the charismatic renewal that began in my hometown of Pittsburgh, Pennsylvania. Not only was I called into a global healing ministry, but I also attended and graduated from what is now an Anglican seminary." Dr. Webb's personal faith, academic credentials, and ministry experience make her an unusually qualified and rare insider-outsider. The consequential subjects she tackles in this volume are not theoretical for her, but very real and deeply understood.

If you are concerned about the spread of Christian nationalism and other political trends affecting the witness of the gospel in the United States and around the world, you will find Dr. Webb's treatment of these issues enormously helpful. The popular adage says, "A problem well-defined is a problem half solved." As Grace Kalisha of the Dell Foundation reminds us, "Albert Einstein is quoted as having said that if he only had an hour to save the world, he would spend 55 minutes defining the problem and only 5 minutes solving it."[1] Dr. Webb has done a little better than Einstein by giving us plenty of material about what's wrong with how Christianity is being misused in the public square, but also plenty of material about how to set it right. Whether you are a pastor, local church lay worker, denominational or institutional executive, organizational leader, academic, or simply a praying believer, you will find this book enormously helpful. But you don't have to be religious at all to appreciate what Dr. Webb provides here. Understanding how Christian nationalists think and act, and the authorities they look to for guidance in changing their opinions, is a crucial step in recognizing that this crisis is indeed formidable and complex, but also solvable. Even if you're not a person of faith, you'll likely develop some after reading Dr. Webb's work!

1. Kalisha, "Problem Well-Defined," para. 1.

One of my great earthly heroes and posthumous spiritual mentors is the young, brave, brilliant World War II–era German church leader Dietrich Bonhoeffer. He demonstrated through his courageous moral resistance to Nazism and Adolf Hitler's dictatorship that the church and faithful Christian people have a unique and incomparable role to play in preserving human freedom and challenging abusive and harmful political power. Church historians often refer to a "Bonhoeffer moment"[2] when people of faith must overtly confront corrupt leaders in the spiritual and temporal realms. Dr. Webb does just that through her excellent critique of the false religion of Christian nationalism, making clear the true Christian message, and exposing the exploitation of that life-giving message by cynical politicians. May we all join her in rising to meet our Bonhoeffer moment as he did his.

Rev. Dr. Rob Schenck
Bishop, the Methodist Evangelical Church in the USA
Visiting Scholar of Christianity and Religious Leadership, the Miller Center for Interreligious Learning and Leadership of Hebrew College, Newton, Massachusetts
Author, *Costly Grace: An Evangelical Minister's Rediscovery of Faith, Hope, and Love* (2018)

2. See, for example, Hale, "Is this a Bonhoeffer Moment?"

Preface

The Apostles' Creed
I believe in God, the Father Almighty,
creator of heaven and earth.
I believe in Jesus Christ, his only Son, our Lord,
who was conceived by the Holy Spirit,
born of the Virgin Mary,
suffered under Pontius Pilate,
was crucified, died, and was buried;
he descended to the dead.
On the third day he rose again;
he ascended into heaven,
is seated at the right hand of the Father,
and will come again to judge the living and the dead.
I believe in the Holy Spirit,
the holy catholic church,
the communion of saints,
the forgiveness of sins,
the resurrection of the body,
and life everlasting.[1]

WHY START WITH THIS creed? Because in response to the query "What think ye of Christ?" early Christians recited a statement of their Christian faith as early as AD 140 at the time of their baptism.

The creed, sometimes called the Roman Creed, points to the heart of the Christian faith and was a summary of what the early apostles believed. Due to adhering to doctrines amidst cultural pressures, heretical beliefs and practices threatened the Christian

1. *United Methodist Hymnal*, 7.

baptismal statement of faith. In AD 325, Christian bishops gathered at the Council of Nicaea—now a ruin in central Turkey—to discuss writing a new creed in order to combat what became known as the Arian heresy. Several versions evolved, and then in AD 385, a more thorough confession of what Christians believe, the Nicene Creed, was approved. A simpler Apostles' Creed evolved over time, during the early centuries of Christianity.

Christians have recited both creeds, along with the Lord's Prayer, during worship for over two thousand years, recounting the story of Christian tradition and catholic (meaning universal) church beliefs. These are the creeds that are foundational to my faith that remind me of its tenets at each worship service I attend.

Today not all those who identify as being Christian follow creedal historic beliefs and practices. Many of them are Pentecostal or charismatic churches focused on healing and speaking in tongues, with prayer and media centers. They believe that we're in a new apostolic age and winning a spiritual war against Satan.

When I interviewed Pastor Bakalov for an article in *Charisma* magazine after attending a Prison Fellowship Conference in Bulgaria in 1999, in our discussion Pastor Bakalov told me that God was "raising up prophets and apostles"[2] and that the old Christianity was no more. His Breakthrough Worship Center had experienced rapid growth and, in so doing, clashed with the more traditional Orthodox and Protestant denominations.

I will be exploring this new apostolic Pentecostal phenomenon as well as its implications because of its popularity in America. Those who are caught up in this new theology and its worship practices run the risk of co-opting and diminishing Christianity. This apostate theology clashes with what evangelicals like me believe. In addition, its leaders consider the ancient liturgy and wordy creeds outdated. With their zeal for finding new and relevant ways of worshiping God, they would do well not to throw out these ancient creeds. My concern will be that in throwing out the baby with the bathwater we are losing the very core of what it means to be a follower of Jesus Christ, the Messiah, who was

2. Webb, "No Longer Underground," 59.

born, crucified, and rose again, sending the Holy Spirit to guide his body, the church, while sitting at the right hand of God to judge the quick and the dead.

Does this mean the same today as it meant yesterday, or is God doing a new thing? Exploring some of Jesus' teachings and actions to see if the current aberrant movement, its extremes, and its dangerous crusader, warlike focus, will help answer this question.

First, I need to confess that I am a born-again believer and follower of Jesus whose spirituality has been enriched through my participation in the charismatic renewal that began in my hometown of Pittsburgh, Pennsylvania. Not only was I called into a global healing ministry, but I also attended and graduated from what is now an Anglican seminary.

Furthermore, I will explore periods of time in church history when church and state became entwined, when Christianity was forced upon the population by political leadership, and when Christians veered away from the compass, the Beatitudes, provided by Jesus and his teachings. The consequences were disastrous. My emphasis will be on recapturing and retelling some of Jesus' teachings and parables as well as reminding us all what is required as followers of Jesus Christ today.

Instead of using the biblical term "kingdom of God," I will instead introduce a new term, the "domain of God," since most Americans do not believe in crowning kings in kingdoms and Jesus did not intend to start an earthly kingdom. He told us as much: "My Kingdom is not an earthly kingdom. If it were, my followers would fight to keep me from being handed over to the Jewish leaders. But my Kingdom is not of this world" (John 18:36, NLT). Instead, Jesus introduced a way of living together in community.

Another way of calling God's domain could be "kin-dom,"[3] since the term emphasizes one of community and loving relationships. I will use this term occasionally. As Christian history has exemplified, Jesus teaches and calls his followers to come together to learn and educate others on what he wants his people to believe and how he wants them to act in any age.

3. Gaines-Cirelli, *Sacred Resistance*, 78n2.

Finally, I will suggest prophetic and strategic actions that might reclaim centuries of Christians' creedal history and ring the alarm about what happens when man's way instead of God's way takes over.

Acknowledgments

SINCE WRITING *FOLLOWING JESUS in the Age of Trumpism*, where I attempted to dialogue—the Braver Angels way—with American Christians, I've become increasingly concerned about the alarming number of American Christians who are under the spell of Christian nationalism,[1] especially the New Apostolic Reformation, as well as the impact Christian Zionism has had on evangelical Christians.

The Holy Spirit has convinced me—during the past two years—that I need to continue to raise awareness of what it means to live and believe the Jesus way. Yet, I pondered, who was I to undertake this task to which I'd been called? Humbly, I prayed. A resounding message came to me to contact the community known as Red Letter Christians, now not only a prophetic presence in America but also in other countries. I'm indebted to the committed members of their community for their help, especially Susan and Kasey, and for the staff of Wipf and Stock for all their support.

Other concerned clergy have helped: the Rev. Dr. Greg Carey, the Rev. Dr. Rob Schenck, Frederick Clarkson of Political Research, John C. Dorhauser, Dr. David Gushee, Dr. Matthew Taylor, pastor John Pavlovitz, and journalist Stephanie McCrummen. I'm in conversations with them and with like-minded organizations, the Baptist Joint Committee for Religious Liberty, Sojourners, Crossroads and Connections, and Vote for the Common Good. I'm grateful for their insights and writings.

1. Miller, "People Are Still Confused."

I credit Dr. William Lawbaugh for giving many hours of his time to proofread and recommend changes to the original *Following Jesus* manuscript. I also am indebted to retired Bishop Stephen Weaver, who with his extensive biblical wisdom and insights, read the first manuscript and provided conceptual depth to my intuitive theological beliefs. I will include much of what I wrote earlier, because citizenship in God's domain as followers of Jesus is central.

We are all in this together to raise the alarm.

My chapter on the Beatitudes as our compass guide was formed in 2018 from a series of lectures led by William Higgins, who was then pastor of the New Providence Mennonite Church.[2] What I found in his humble lectures was a treasure trove of theological insight. Even though the Beatitudes are central to Anabaptist theology, they have somehow gotten lost in our secular culture. The Beatitudes Compass, as I have classified them, form the central core of what it means for Christians to follow on the Jesus pathway.

2. Now a teacher for LMC, a fellowship of Anabaptist churches.

PART I

Introducing God's Plan

1

The Roman Empire

For God loved the world so much that he gave his only Son.

—JOHN 3:16 (GNT)

SO WHY DID GOD choose this time in the world's history, the age of the domination of the Roman Empire, to be born into the world as a human and live among his chosen people in the land of Judea, Samaria, and Galilee? Despite how corrupt life in the occupied countries of the Roman Empire then was, God loved his people! He needed to show them how he wanted them to behave under the authority and rule of that political reality.

The Roman Empire[1] had been a republic since 509 BC when the Romans overthrew the Etruscans. The new Roman Republic not only subdued all their rivals but deployed its soldiers to keep the peace and quell any uprising. At first, the republic was ruled by a series of triumvirates. Mark Antony and Octavian fought and defeated two of them. When Mark Antony committed suicide, Octavian became the sole leader of the Roman Republic and gave himself the name Emperor or Caesar Augustus.

1. Several sources informed my discussion of the Roman Empire that follows, including Wikipedia, "Herod the Great"; History.com, "Ancient Rome"; Ushistory.org, "Roman Republic"; and Connolly, *Jews in the Time.*

Under Augustus's reign, the Roman Empire exemplified a model of peace and prosperity, known as the Pax Romana, that lasted from 27 BC to AD 180. Yet half of those who lived in the Roman Empire were slaves—some because they were captured by Roman soldiers, while others could not pay their debts and became slaves. Even though Romans were engineering geniuses at building roads and aqueducts, they had not yet mastered sanitary living conditions in their crowded cities and villages. Sewage spewed stench and disease. Life was tough. Sickness and death were ever-present. Their many gods were capricious and needed to be appeased. A variety of philosophies and mystery religions existed.

Around the time of Jesus' birth, subjects called Caesar Augustus savior. He saved them from the chaos that Rome had been and ushered in a golden age of prosperity with a forced peace. He issued imperial proclamations called "gospel" or good news. To most, those proclamations were bad for a depressed and rebellious people. Legions of soldiers marched through towns and villages, killing all who resisted arrest. Even towns like Magdala, a few miles from Nazareth, were destroyed in 52 BC, about fifty years before Jesus' birth.

The territory of Palestine presented certain challenges to keeping the peace. First, Rome divided Palestine into separate fiefdoms: Idumea, Judea, Samaria, Galilee, and Assyria west of the Jordan River, and the ten cities called the Decapolis to the east. Most in the territory were Abraham's descendants and believed in one God. And although they were conquered many times, they longed to be their own masters. From 103 BC on, revolts and potential uprisings were a constant threat while Rome set up and dethroned kings in each of its conquered territories. Crosses dotted every highway and byway. When Antiochus IV, King of Assyria, tried to get the Jewish people to change their religious practices to Greek forms, the Maccabees revolted. At that time, a Maccabean family, the Hasmoneans, ruled Judea.

Emperor Augustus appointed Herod as prefect for Judea in 37 BC, but Herod called himself king even though he was appointed governor. He was part Idumaean, yet Herod's allegiance was to Rome. After proclaiming himself king, Herod executed forty-five Sadducees, confiscated their property, and built fortresses to secure his kingship.

Besides not liking to bow down to foreign occupiers, most Jewish people had mixed feelings about King Herod. They had their own religious/political system and resented being at the will of corrupt Roman rulers who worshiped an emperor. For the Roman government to keep the peace, they made a pact with the Jewish people to not interfere with their religious traditions of worshiping only one God and allowed them to keep their holy holidays. Rome's responsibility under the pact was to secure peace and punish any individual or group that attempted to overthrow the Roman government.

Herod was a wheeler and dealer with many wives. In his reign, his anger raged, and his siblings and adult children plotted against each other. Yet, he succeeded in building an aqueduct near the port of Caesarea, and, more importantly, rebuilt the temple in Jerusalem. During the last few years before his death, Herod became more paranoid, and his mood alternated between rampages of killing to rampages of building. At least his Jewish subjects liked their new temple and the aqueduct that brought water. Before his death, Herod changed his will to give his kingdom to three of his sons. After his death, Emperor Tiberius recognized his wishes but gave each son a different territory to rule, to deal with sibling infighting.

The following is a clear explanation of the political situation under the Herodian kings:

> Herod the Great was a half-Jewish hybrid king who had spilled blood all over the land through slavery, slaughter, and war. He wasn't well-loved, especially by the Jews. Feeling continually threatened by his sons' insatiable appetite for wealth and power and jealous pursuit of the throne, Herod killed his own kids. He even had one of them drowned in the royal pool. He died just after Jesus was born, around 4 BC. After his death three of Herod's surviving sons—Archelaus, Antipas, and Philip—fought for the throne, and the Jewish people were once again

> stuck in a royal mess. When the boys took their case to Rome the Jews sent a delegation to protest, declaring that they had had enough of the Herod clan and didn't want any of these boys as their king. The Roman emperor didn't listen to the protest and instead divided the kingdom among the Herod family, giving them less to botch things up. . . . Archelaus got Judea and Jerusalem and Antipas got Galilee. He ditched his wife and married his brother's wife, Herodias.[2]

The Pharisees, Herodians, and Sadducees held positions of political and religious authority and power. There were other groups such as the Great Sanhedrin, the Jewish high court, as well as the scribes and lawyers who debated before the judges. The Herodians were a political party that supported the Herodian dynasty, thereby accommodating Roman rule for their own self-enhancement, probably making deals for all kinds of favors. But the Pharisees stood for Jewish independence. The Jewish people, just trying to make ends meet and pay their taxes, were compliant, rebellious, or scared.

Aptly, this period of history has been called "the perfect storm"[3] or a clash of who to worship as lord of all. Caesar was to be called "lord" and worshiped; the Jewish people, anticipating the coming of their Messiah as their lord, pleaded for God to send the Messiah to rescue them from their Roman rulers. Their very existence was being challenged. With Jewish political groups vying for influence, Rome was rapidly losing its patience with the recalcitrant Jewish people.

So, God decided to send his son, to be born of Mary as Jesus—a different kind of savior, a different kind of ruler—to show his people a different way of living.

2. Claiborne and Haw, *Jesus for President*, 77–78.

3. Wright, *Simply Jesus*, ch. 3 (title).

2

God Sends Jesus

In our culture, we remember Jesus' birth on December 25. But most likely he was not born in the winter but in the late summer or fall. Scholars have speculated that his birth was around 4–6 BC.[1] He was born into the Jewish Davidic line of ancestry through Joseph. His parents gave him the name Jesus, or Joshua, or bar-Joseph, son of Joseph. His real father is God, who, with the Holy Spirit, makes up the Holy Trinity or Godhead with Jesus, called Son of Man or Son of God. The name Jesus was a derivative of Joshua (Yahweh saves), known as a Jewish warrior who would restore the glory of his people. Jesus—he "who is, and who was, and who is to come" (Rev 1:4 NIV)—came not as a warrior but as a preacher, priest, healer, and shepherd to live among his people, or as believers who attend Holy Communion might say, "Christ has died. Christ is risen, Christ will come again."[2]

For Catholic and Orthodox Christians, *Theotokos* signifies the infant Mary. God chose Mary to be the mother of God's son. Mary's parents were a devout Jewish couple who, like Abraham and his wife Sarah, had been childless for many years. At each Jewish festival they attended in Jerusalem, they prayed that God would favor them with a child. Mary's mother, Anna, believed, like all Jewish

1. Wikipedia, "Date of the Birth," para. 1.
2. Episcopal Church, *Book of Common Prayer*, 363.

women of her day, that she was worthless if she could not get pregnant. Mary began to ponder the things that her mother told her, particularly about what a joy and a blessing her birth had been for them and how much God loved her. Her parents taught her above all else to trust God, who makes impossible things happen. From reading the prophets she learned that God favors poor people, widows, orphans, and virgins.

Saints Anna and Joachim with the infant Mary.
This icon is from my personal collection.

If you belong to a Pentecostal or a charismatic church, you may not appreciate icons and dismiss these ancient Christian traditions. But you probably remember Mary at Christmas, because of the manger scene that we see so often in Christmas pageants.

Some churches invite the community to view a live nativity scene at Christmas time. Angels sing and shepherds gather on chilly winter evenings in Advent—the liturgical season before Christmas. At a Mennonite church in Lancaster, Pennsylvania, volunteers usher visitors into a barn to adore the scene of Mary and Joseph and their newborn baby with farm animals standing nearby. Observers sit on a ball of straw and ponder the miraculous event.

This Orthodox icon has a prominent spot on my living room wall. It illustrates Jesus' birth by showing Mary and Joseph and their newborn in a cave. Yet, Jesus might have been born in a simple Bethlehem dwelling. Biblical scholars researched and archaeologists pinpointed an underground ruin in Jerusalem that appears to be a possible home of that period. The dwelling existed on three levels. On the upper level, guests slept; on the middle level, meals were prepared and family members gathered and probably slept; on the lower level, overflow guests stayed and animals were brought in at nighttime. Probably the upper-level guest rooms were occupied when pregnant Mary arrived, so Mary and Joseph were ushered into the lower-level guest room. Here is where "the Word became flesh and [began to dwell] among us" (John 1:14 NIV).

Icon of the Nativity. I inherited this wall icon from my father.

In this Orthodox Christmas icon, Jesus' face appears more like a man's than an infant's. Mary rests nearby while the womenfolk below tend to the baby's needs. Meanwhile, Joseph sits off in a corner, perhaps wondering how he fits into the grand scheme of things. How many times have fathers felt this way when their wives give birth?

Miracle of miracles. Whether in a barn, a cave, or a basement guest room, the omnipotent, invisible, unapproachable God enters into the world as a human baby, to touch and be touched, to see and be seen, to hear and be heard, to love and be loved, and, when he became a man, to show his people how to live as participants in a different kind of way of life.

Before Jesus' birth, Mary and Joseph traveled to Bethlehem, Joseph's birthplace, to take part in the census issued by Quirinius, then appointed the governor of Assyria, during the height of the Roman Empire. The census was unpopular, especially among priests, and led to the rise of the Zealots, who despised Roman domination and revolted.

3

Early Challenges

MAYBE A YEAR OR so after Jesus' birth, Joseph decided to take his young family and flee to Egypt, responding to a dream and afraid of what might happen to his infant son because of Herod's—then king of Judea—increasing madness and jealousy after learning about a newly born king from the wise men from the east who came to bring him gifts. Matthew records what Herod decided to do to protect his kingship: "When Herod saw that he had been tricked by the wise men, he was infuriated, and he sent and killed all the children in and around Bethlehem who were two years old or under, according to the time that he had learned from the wise men" (Matt 2:16–18 NRSVA). Their cries haunt us whenever young children are killed by guns today.

Scholars have determined that Herod died after Jesus' birth and before Joseph, Mary, and Jesus returned from Egypt.[1] With Archelaus, one of Herod's sons, ruling Judea with his propensity toward violence, Joseph decided to return and settle in Nazareth in Galilee, now ruled by Herod Antipas, who was the lesser of two evil heirs of Herod.

During his childhood, Jesus lived with his family in Nazareth, attended synagogue, and memorized and studied the psalms, the prophets, and the history of his Jewish ancestry. About four

1. Kraybill, *Upside-Down Kingdom*, 50.

hundred conservative Jewish peasant families lived in this town, located in hill country about twelve miles from the Sea of Galilee. Many were farmers who struggled to exist while attempting to pay their taxes on time and taking care of each other. The town was within walking distance of the nearby wealthy Greek city of Sepphoris, where the throne of Herod Antipas was located. When he was a teenager, Jesus undoubtedly walked with Joseph, who practiced carpentry, over to Sepphoris to help him in the construction of houses for wealthy Roman citizens, many with decorated ceramic floors, some still preserved to this day.

Jesus' ministry started when he was about thirty years old. First, Jesus survived temptations and testing in the wilderness, submitted to baptism by his cousin John in the Jordan River (Matt 3:13, Mark 1:9, Luke 3:21), then returned to Nazareth to begin his ministry.

One Sabbath day, he was chosen to read the selected Scripture from the Torah in the synagogue. He read this chosen passage from the prophet Isaiah:

> The Spirit of the Lord is upon me, because the Lord has anointed me. He has sent me to preach good news to the poor, to proclaim release to the prisoners and recovery of sight to the blind, to liberate the oppressed, and to proclaim the year of the Lord's favor. (Isa 61:1–2, as recorded in Luke 4:18–19 CEB)

After reading only a portion from the selected reading, Jesus rolled up the scroll, returned it to the attendant, and announced the service. That may have been why some of the parishioners in the synagogue that day were so angry. After the service, they tried to throw Jesus off a cliff, their anger intensified by what he didn't read. The reaction of his neighbors became the first challenge that Jesus faced in fulfilling his mission.

But when Jesus began attracting large crowds of followers, the authorities took notice. At first his healings on the Sabbath and his claims to have divine authority caused discussions and concern among the Pharisees. Then came the overturning of the commercial enterprisers' tables in the temple courtyard. That infuriated the religious leaders, who went to Pilate and tried to convince him that Jesus was a rabble-rouser and a disturber of the peace.

Jesus' awful human challenges followed, beginning in the garden at night. There, when his friends were asleep after their meal, the anticipated pain wrenched his heart, and his gut felt fear. Large drops like a bloody sweat fell to the ground as he prayed, perhaps crying out, "Please, Father God, take the pain away! Please, Father God, I don't want to go through with it! Please, Father God, isn't there a way out?"

Why couldn't his friends understand? Why wouldn't the religious leaders hear the truth? What about his family? Why couldn't God choose someone else to do this dirty work? He prayed the night through on his knees.

Just before dawn, soldiers came to take him away. Jesus submitted to his Father's will. He looked up from his prayers as Judas, his dinner companion and one of his trusted friends, kissed his cheek then turned, nodding his head to the waiting soldiers. Jesus let the soldiers blindfold him and take him to Annas, the High Priest's home. Then he stood still as guards took turns hitting him while they waited for Annas to appear. Each time the soldiers hit Jesus, they taunted him to guess which one of them was doing the beating.

First, Annas interrogated Jesus; next, Annas's son-in-law, Caiaphas; then, the members of the Sanhedrin. Seventy of the top Jewish religious and political leaders encircled Jesus and spat in his face. Some of them also took turns hitting him. After this physical and verbal abuse, soldiers tossed him down the steep wooden steps into a dank, windowless underground room. Jesus rested on its cold, damp stone floor, his body only beginning to feel the pain. Perhaps he prepared himself by drawing crosses with his own blood.[2]

Early in the morning, the heavy door opened. Jesus was bound and led up the steps and out across the paved roads past still-sleeping homes to Pilate's Roman mansion. There the inquisition continued.

2. I visited the proposed room and saw the markings on the wall.

Pilate sent him on to Herod. The frustrated Herod, probably having awakened with a hangover and feeling guilty about John the Baptist's death, screamed at Jesus. He threw his royal robe at Jesus and sent him back to Pilate.

A foot-weary, bruised, and confused Jesus stood again before Pilate. Still finding no legal reason to put Jesus to death, Pilate decided to order the soldiers to whip Jesus instead. Maybe that would satisfy the Sanhedrin and get them off his back, he may have thought. Soldiers whipped prisoners with strands of three ropes embedded with sharp stones and bits of metal. Sometimes prisoners did not survive the whipping. The captains of the palace guard tested young recruits of the garrison of soldiers stationed in Jerusalem for their courage by seeing if they could whip prisoners without flinching themselves. The prisoners usually screamed, and blood sprayed everywhere.

Jesus took the whipping without crying out. After it was over, he lay on the paved courtyard, near death. One soldier carefully helped him up to sit on a nearby stone. Another put the royal robe back on to cover the bloody mess they had made of his back. Others, showing off their bravado, spat on him and taunted him. Roman soldiers called this sport "The King's Game."[3] Soldiers rolled dice to see who would get to put the crown of thorns on his head. The soldier who rolled the highest die pushed the thorn points deep down into Jesus' scalp. Blood dripped into his eyes.

The crowd's turn was next. The soldiers, now having to hold up the badly bruised and bleeding body of Jesus, pushed him to the edge of the balcony. All eyes turned to look as Pilate asked the crowd if they wanted him to release "this King of the Jews" for them.

Conversation ceased. People caught their breath. They did not know what to make of seeing Jesus beaten, dazed, and bloody. Agitators in their midst yelled, "Crucify him!"

Roman soldiers led Jesus back to the barracks, where they ripped off the robe that stuck to his bloody back. Then, they led

3. This was suggested by tour guides on my Jerusalem pilgrimage to visit the site.

him away with the rest of the prisoners to the place of crucifixion. Jesus fell twice from loss of blood. His head throbbed from the thorns in his scalp. Mixed emotions of terror and anger may have screamed throughout his body. He shivered from pain and loss of body fluids.

It was worse when they reached the place of crucifixion. After laying him flat on the crossed trees on the ground, the soldiers pounded nails into his feet and hands. Then they divided his clothes among themselves. The sun beat hot on Jesus' head as the soldiers lifted the cross. It hurt to breathe, and he began to suffocate. His worst moment of shame occurred when he felt that God had completely abandoned him.

At the sixth hour, the soldiers declared him dead. His agony and shame were over, just in time for the new day of the domain of God he taught about to begin.

PART II

God's Domain

4

Christians Suffer

JESUS APPEARED TO MANY after his death and told his disciples that he would send the Holy Spirit (we remember this as the Day of Pentecost) to usher in the age of the church. But the new age promised to be no picnic. Newly converted Christians were subjected to torture, persecution, beheading, or crucifixion just like Jesus. Even though Jesus tried to prepare his disciples that if they followed him, they would suffer, it didn't sink in right away. Jesus asked his disciples if they were willing to endure what he was about to suffer.

During the first two centuries after Jesus' death and resurrection, while the Holy Spirit was guiding them after their Pentecostal experience, Jesus' apostles and many followers anticipated Jesus' imminent return. During that time new Christians endured being arrested, jailed, beaten, and sent to the gladiators to be trampled to death by wild animals.

Each succeeding Roman emperor tried everything to get rid of the Jesus cult, but, instead, the example of their love for each other, their zeal for their faith, and their courage kept attracting new converts. They lived together and worshiped together, taking care of widows and orphans, attracting both slaves and Roman citizens to join their underground movement, eventually becoming known as Christ followers.

Today, since we are disciples of Jesus, we Christians must expect some emotional and physical suffering. Most of us American Christians have only a vague concept of what that is all about. But Christians who lived during the time of Rome's capricious ways experienced that kind of suffering because they refused to renounce their allegiance to their Lord Jesus Christ. Instead, their allegiance was to him and not to the ruling emperor. In AD 70, under Emperor Nero, they were even accused of starting the fire that almost destroyed Rome.

Almost all of Jesus' twelve apostles suffered hardships and were killed: King Herod Agrippa had James, John's brother, killed. He arrested Peter and put him in jail (Acts 12), but Peter miraculously escaped, only to be crucified upside down later in Rome after supporting the underground church during Nero's reign. Andrew, meanwhile, was able to spread the good news about Jesus in regions of Russia, Turkey, and Greece but was crucified after a severe beating (like Jesus) in Greece. Thomas was stabbed with a spear in India during one of his missionary trips while he was planting churches. Matthew, alias Levi, was killed by a sword wound while in Ethiopia. Bartholomew, alias Nathanael, when preaching in Armenia, was flayed to death with a whip. Philip was either beheaded or crucified in Hierapolis. When he refused to denounce his faith in Jesus, Thaddeus was thought to have been killed with arrows. Matthias, chosen to replace Judas Iscariot, who committed suicide after betraying Jesus, was stoned to death and then beheaded. Only John, the beloved disciple, after miraculously surviving being boiled in hot oil and being imprisoned in a dungeon on Patmos, then becoming bishop, escaped the martyrdom of the other apostles by dying of old age![1]

Paul warned new Christians to expect suffering and persecution (1 Thess 3:3–4; Rom 8:17–18; 2 Tim 3:12). He endured imprisonment, being whipped, and being stoned; finally, Nero had him beheaded.

Today, in countries where there has been consistent government persecution of Christians, such as in North Korea, Iran,

1. See St. Matthews Episcopal Church, "How the Apostles Died."

China, India, Pakistan, and Nigeria, reports indicate that Christianity is growing. In addition, like the early Christians suffering under the cruelty of the Romans, today's Christians in these countries endure threats, intimidation, and depravities.

The suffering and trials of Christians throughout the ages kept alive the real gospel that immortalizes Jesus' words of reassurance and love—not the demands of kings and rulers—so that all people have an opportunity to hear the real good news.

5

Follow a Compass: The Beatitudes

When Jesus gathered his followers together, he gave them compass directions—what has become known as the Beatitudes. I have studied and prayed over them to discern how we might apply them in the twenty-first century. I'm indebted to the scholarship of William Higgins and Jim Forrest,[1] and to the lives of other Christians who, by their example, have lived their lives as followers of Jesus.

Eight Beatitudes are found in the Gospel of Matthew (5:3–12) at the beginning of the Sermon on the Mount and summarized into five in the Gospel of Luke (6:20b–23) in what has become known as the Sermon on the Plain. Jesus' sermon points gave his followers good orderly directions.

Markarios, the Greek word, in English becomes *beatitude* and means the same as being especially praised by God if one demonstrates these qualities in one's daily life. According to Jonathan Pennington's new theological commentary on Matt 5–7, they are "declared observation[s] about a way of being in the world."[2] They express a kind of wisdom similar to Proverbs that a parent might say to an upset child who is having a tough time at school or losing an important sports game. *Chill out. Sometimes you lose. Sometimes you win. It's the way you play the game that counts.*

1. Forrest, *Ladder of the Beatitudes.*
2. Quoted in Hill, "Strange New World," para. 5.

When bad situations occur in our lives, we think we deserve better, especially if we're Christians. Aren't we entitled to wealth, prosperity, and admiration? But that's not God's way, as Jesus teaches in the Beatitudes and illustrates through his parables and healings.

Pastor William Higgins describes the Beatitudes in the context of the ancient literary structure of parallels.[3] For this reason, I will discuss the first eight in his format, putting the first and third together, then the second and fourth together.

BLESSED ARE THE POOR IN SPIRIT FOR THEIRS IS THE KINGDOM OF HEAVEN

When Matthew writes "poor in spirit," Luke writes just "poor" in the first beatitude. The Hebrew word for "poor" in Matthew and Isaiah, *anawim*, are the same. In both cases, Jesus really meant the poor, the hungry, the destitute. He reminds members of the synagogue congregation of this when he reads from the prophet Isaiah. Those who heard could identify their present time with the suffering of their ancestors in exile in Babylon, remembering how they had been driven like cattle by the Babylonian army away from their homeland into captivity. Now, they were once again captives, in Rome, this time in their own land, their hopes not yet realized.

The Greek word "poor" in the Gospel of Luke literally means without resources or desperate, like Jonah when he found himself in the belly of the big fish and cried out to God for help. Those who lose all their early possessions in a flood, a fire, or an earthquake and have no insurance or other resources to cover their losses understand this meaning; as do those who become addicted to a drug or a behavior that pulls them down. They experience blessedness when they are willing to reach out for help by calling a hotline phone number or attending a recovery meeting.

3. Higgins, classes taught at New Providence Mennonite Church, Lancaster, 2018.

BLESSED ARE THE MEEK, FOR THEY SHALL INHERIT THE EARTH

The word "meek," the same Hebrew word, *anawim*, used in the third beatitude (Matthew), can also mean humble, gentle, or even powerless. The same meaning appears in Ps 37. Make the most of it, the psalmist writes; "Be still before the Lord and wait patiently for him; do not fret when men succeed in their evil ways, when they carry out their wicked schemes" (Ps 37:7 NIV) This psalm reflects—despite what the world says or does—that followers of Jesus need to continue to serve those in desperate need, with actions such as rebuilding and restoring after a hurricane disaster and protecting refugees who came seeking asylum in America and are now facing deportation or imprisonment. We may have to put up with misfortune, trials, and tribulations, but we know who we are, made in God's image. We rest assured that God is with us and will never forsake us.

One of my spiritual directors encouraged me to go on a silent retreat with the task of meditating on the word "humble" or "meek." God taught me during that retreat humility does not mean humiliation but finding and claiming my actual self, as distinguished from my damaged self, or trying to fulfill the expectation of others. Humility means trusting that God has made each of us unique and special as his child.

Thomas à Kempis wrote,

> It is the humble man whom God protects and liberates; it is the humble whom He loves and consoles. To the humble He turns and upon them he bestows grace, that after their humiliation He may raise them up to glory. He reveals his secrets to the humble and with kind invitation bids them come to Him. Thus the humble man enjoys peace in the midst of many vexations, because his trust is in God, not in the world.[4]

4. Thomas à Kempis, *Imitation of Christ*, 37.

The humble man or woman receives God's special honor and a proclamation from the heavenly throne, "Well done good and faithful servant" (Matt 25:21 RSV).

BLESSED ARE THOSE WHO MOURN FOR THEY SHALL BE COMFORTED

Jesus' Jewish followers were in a state of mourning. When Joseph returned from Egypt after Herod's death, there must have been mourning and lamentation. As previously noted, just before his death, Herod had ordered all children under the age of two in Bethlehem and environs to be slaughtered.

When Jesus taught this second beatitude to those gathered around him on the mountain or the plain, he recalled the book of Lamentations; his listeners mourned their time of exile in Babylon while also mourning their dead children under Rome's subjugation.

We mourn and grieve over life today, wanting it the way it used to be. Perhaps you've been laid off from a job because your place of employment is downsizing or going out of business, or you've been trying to survive from losing your government job. Perhaps one of your children has died of an opiate overdose. Perhaps you're feeling mistreated or misunderstood, and you resent that the world seems to be passing you by. At some time in our lives, we will experience deep sorrow and loss. Along with our feelings of loss, we'll be angry.

Many of Jesus' followers were angry. They had been anticipating that once again the land would be theirs. But now they were subjects of the Roman Empire. They were angry at the loss of friends or family members, many killed by Herod or crucified by Roman soldiers because of their revolt.

Revolution seethed in Jewish bones and sinew. God's creation was on the verge of destruction and that called, they believed, for extraordinary measures. But God decided to live, teach, and transform his people into the true royal way, with the Beatitudes as their guide.

Jesus weeps with us when we mourn. He wept when his friend Lazarus died. He mourned when he entered Jerusalem with foreknowledge of the destruction of the temple yet again. He mourned because he foresaw the dangers his disciples would face in a hostile world: wars, famines, and persecutions.

He still mourns with us today. His presence and face appeared to me one night about thirty years ago. I had been attending and presenting at a pastoral care conference in Washington, DC, when my sister died. We had been estranged. She had refused to speak to me for about ten years. A member of her family called to tell me not to attend her funeral. In fact, the local police had been told to arrest me if I showed up. Devastated and in a state of profound mourning, Jesus' face appeared for a brief second, comforting me.

Pastoral counselors like me, who have experienced loss and have been alienated in our families or in society, have been given a gift of empathy for those who mourn. We identify with the sorrow and suffering of others in the name of Jesus and become part of the healing process of those who are hurting. With Jesus, we empathize with those who experience sorrow and suffering.

Those who seek to follow the way of Jesus strive to help the poor and the lowly. A friend recently told me about the time she and another friend were partners at her parish's foot-washing at a homeless shelter. She loved listening to her minister talk about ministering to those less fortunate, just like Jesus.

BLESSED ARE THOSE WHO HUNGER AND THIRST FOR RIGHTEOUSNESS, FOR THEY SHALL BE SATISFIED

Righteousness comes from the Greek word *dikaiosune.* The word also means justice and the state of being justified. Righteousness is the opposite of covetousness, what the tenth commandment prohibits. Jesus calls his followers to be hungry for justice, recognizing that the Jews longed for a leader who would bring back justice and fairness. For us today, we long for a leader who cares about righteousness. As the psalmist states, "He [God] will make your innocence radiate like the dawn, and the justice of your cause like the noonday sun" (Ps 37:6 NLT).

But that's not fair! How come he gets away with it? Many of us have experienced this child's sense of unfairness when one thinks she's being punished and another sibling is not. All those who experience injustice or unfairness desire justice and cry out similarly, *That's not fair!*

African Americans or immigrants far too often do not find justice in American courts because they may not have the financial resources to hire attorneys for their defense, especially when they have been falsely accused. Those suffering from mental illnesses or addiction are ostracized and shamed by society.

Jim Forrest writes about an Orthodox nun, Mother Maria Skobtsova, who was born into an aristocratic family in Riga, Latvia. After fleeing from Bolshevik persecution to France, she dedicated her life to providing care, assistance, and protection to Russian refugees in the 1930s and then for Jews in 1942, smuggling Jewish children out of France in garbage bins. When arrested in 1943, she was sent to Ravensbrück. She chose to take the place of another prisoner sentenced to be shot. She writes,

> There is one moment when you start burning with love and you have the inner desire to throw yourself at the feet of some other human being. This one moment is enough. Immediately you know that instead of losing your life, it is being given back to you twofold.[5]

The monastic order that she founded encapsulated the same social praxis espoused by Reinhold Niebuhr and codified in the Serenity Prayer, especially the courage to change the injustices of this world.

> God grant me the Serenity
> to accept the things I cannot change,
> the Courage to change the things I can
> and the Wisdom to know the difference.
> Living one day at a time;
> enjoying one moment at a time;

5. Forest, *Ladder of the Beatitudes*, 72.

> accepting hardship as the pathway to peace.
> Taking this sinful world as it is,
> not as I would have it,
> trusting that he will make all things right,
> if I surrender to his will.
> That I may be reasonably happy in this life,
> and supremely happy with him forever in the next.[6]

Many psalms describe the Lord approving the godly or righteous and hating the wicked and those who do violence (Ps 11:5). In Proverbs, memories of the righteous are blessed but the names of the wicked will rot (Prov 10:7).

Jesus probably memorized many of the psalms and proverbs. When he taught the Beatitudes in the Sermon on the Mount or the Plain, he was just rephrasing them. He illustrated them in his parables.

Our attitude should not be just craving justice but advocating for it. Our cries go up to the Father as an intercessor so that God will bring justice to pass in his time.

BLESSED ARE THE MERCIFUL FOR THEY WILL RECEIVE MERCY

In this fifth beatitude, the Hebrew word for mercy is *khesed* and can be translated as tenderness, loving kindness, graciousness, self-giving, or unconditional love. The Greek word *eleos*, and also *eleemosyne*, means merciful giving or giving alms. Works of mercy mean caring for others, especially those who are usually discriminated against.

Mary praised God for his mercy when she sang the Magnificat:

> My soul magnifies the Lord
> and my spirit rejoices in God my Savior,
> for He has looked with favor on the lowliness of his servant.
> Surely, from now on all generations will call me blessed;
> for the Mighty One has done great things for me,

6. Quoted in Webb, *Tree of Renewed Life*, 28–29, in a chapter on the origins of the prayer.

and holy is his name.
His mercy is for those who fear him
from generation to generation.
He has shown strength with his arm;
He has scattered the proud in the thoughts of their hearts.
He has brought down the powerful from their thrones,
and lifted up the lowly;
He has filled the hungry with good things,
and sent the rich away empty.
He has helped his servant Israel,
in remembrance of his mercy,
according to the promise He made to our ancestors,
to Abraham and to his descendants forever.
(Luke 1:46–55 NRSVA)

If we're merciful to others, God will be merciful to us. We've heard the saying, "Do unto others as you would have others do unto you." That's essentially what this beatitude means. Being merciful involves more than just feeding the hungry and clothing the naked—although these are required for Christians—it also means forgiveness when someone has done you wrong. Jesus repeated this way of living to his disciples repeatedly, sometimes almost with frustration or citing the words from the prophet Micah, though they should have memorized them in Hebrew 101: "And what does the Lord require of you? To act justly and to love mercy and to walk humbly with your God" (Mic 6:8 NIV).

To emphasize the point, Jesus told a parable about settling accounts (Matt 18:23–35). A lender wanted one of his servants to repay a large debt, but the servant pleaded for forgiveness of his debt and the lender agreed. The amount of payment in the story, 10,000 talents, would be billions of dollars today. The annual tax income from Herod's whole kingdom was about 900 talents. Maybe the lender's servant was a tax collector for Herod. A tax collector would be commissioned to collect larger amounts in taxes than was required to turn over to his Roman overseer. Often poor people could not pay the required taxes, and then the tax collector didn't have the amount needed to meet his required allotment of taxes. If this situation occurred and he was unable to pay, the servant would have been sold into slavery or worse. But according to the parable, instead of arresting the tax collector, the overseer or lender showed mercy. However, his servant did not show the same kind of mercy to someone who owed him money and couldn't pay his debt. The point of this story: God expects us to show the same kind of mercy to others as has been shown to us by sending Jesus to take our sins upon the cross—thus exonerating us from suffering the consequences of our sins.

What happens when we don't pay our taxes every year? Sometimes we receive notices of fines. Then we go before the local IRS office to plead our case. Cheating on reporting our taxes or depositing illegally acquired funds into offshore accounts occurs commonly. Still, the one who cheats in this way can be fined or sent to jail. The overseer or lender in the parable showed the same mercy we hope that the IRS will show us when we appeal an IRS decision; otherwise, we pay a fine or go to jail.

How many times have you felt that when someone has given you a generous gift you needed to pay them back by reciprocating? Instead, if we follow Jesus, we need to accept the gift graciously and show the same compassion and generosity to someone else in similar need. And our almsgiving needs to be generous because God is forgiving and generous.

BLESSED ARE THE PURE IN HEART FOR THEY WILL SEE GOD

In this sixth beatitude, pure in heart equates to having the right motives. The Greek word *katharos* means anyone without any stain or impurity who is truthful, has integrity, and has a clean heart. The Pharisees had an easy life due to their position in society. They wanted everyone to know how pious they were, but Jesus was quick to point out to his disciples their hypocrisy.

> The teachers of the law and the Pharisees sit in Moses' seat. So, you must be careful to do everything they tell you. But do not do what they do, for they do not practice what they preach. They tie up heavy, cumbersome

> loads and put them on other people's shoulders, but they themselves are not willing to lift a finger to move them. Everything they do is done for people to see: They make their phylacteries wide and the tassels on their garments long; they love the place of honor at banquets and the most important seats in the synagogues; they love to be greeted with respect in the marketplaces and to be called "Rabbi" by others. (Matt 23:1–7 NIV)

Jesus even called Pharisees "whitewashed tombs" (Matt 23:27 NET), meaning showy on the outside and dead on the inside. They certainly did not have the right motives. Neither do we when we show our piety in public, for example going around with ashes on our foreheads at the beginning of Lent or allowing our names to be put in various publications indicating how much money we have donated to this or that charity. To follow Jesus means we keep our focus on God, act with integrity, and, as much as possible, give anonymously with humble generosity.

How we each look forward to seeing God face to face! We remember Paul's words in his letter to the church in Corinth: "For now we see in a mirror dimly, but then face to face. Now I know in part. Then I shall understand fully, even as I have been fully understood" (1 Cor 13:12 RSV).

Moses desired to see God's face, but God told him that no one can see God and live. Even when Jesus was transfigured before Peter, James, and John, they were terrified, as if blinded by the brilliance of the light. A cloud passed over them just as a cloud covered Moses' face so he couldn't see God, only hear him. Elijah heard God in a still small voice but didn't actually see God.

Envision the throne of God; imagine a brilliant light, so brilliant native earthly eyes are almost blinded by the light's intensity. To be in the presence of God will fill us with such pure joy and love, the same kind of love so artistically shown in the book and movie *The Shack*. William Young shows the persons of the Trinity in the same radiating love between them as God has for us, just as we are drawn up into their union in the icon the Holy Trinity—the kind of love that warms your heart and does not let you go.

BLESSED ARE THE PEACEMAKERS, FOR THEY SHALL BE CALLED CHILDREN OF GOD

In this seventh beatitude, Jesus blessed peacemakers as special children of God. Roman emperors called themselves peacemakers. Romans thought of themselves as keepers of peace. But they did so by force of arms, enslaving those they conquered.

In the United States, we spend almost half our federal budget on maintaining our military might. We call the biggest nuclear weapon in our arsenal of weapons "the Peacekeeper" and have the largest military-industrial complex in the world, selling more weapons than any other country, having more nuclear weapons than any other country—the equivalent of over 150 Hiroshima bombs—enough to destroy the world ten times over. There are forty-nine Minuteman bombs in Colorado alone[7] and our current administration wants to build more and to test them.

Today America's current federal government voted to spend 150 billion dollars in additional funding for national defense. This funding is intended to be allocated across various areas, including shipbuilding, a Golden Dome missile defense system, munitions production, as well as investments in nuclear forces, air superiority, and the defense industrial base.

We don't need more ships or more tanks. Drones are cheaper to build, but they still kill. Peacemakers try diplomacy to solve disputes between nations. If we Americans are opposed to other countries having nuclear weapons, why not set an example for them by eliminating all our nuclear weapons?

Remember the warning former General Eisenhower gave:

> In the councils of government, we must guard against the acquisition of unwarranted influence, whether sought or unsought, by the military-industrial complex. The potential for the disastrous rise of misplaced power exists and will persist.[8]

7. Claiborne and Haw, *Jesus for President*, 178.

8. Eisenhower, "Quotes," sec. War/Defense.

Peacekeepers are liberators, life givers, not avengers with weapons. America has a reputation for taking life, not protecting life. We export more weapons than any other country and we are the only civilized nation to still practice the death penalty.

Many of my friends and family members love to watch and discuss the latest football game, particularly on Super Bowl Sunday. This violent sport causes brain concussions and other lifelong injuries, yet the NFL and its high-salaried players dominate the sports news. I choose not to watch football because the game reminds me of gladiator matches in Roman coliseums,[9] where many courageous Christians fought wild beasts or gladiators. Romans who followed—almost religiously—those grotesque spectacles bear a similarity to American football fanatics. The NFL players who kneel during the singing of the National Anthem challenge our preoccupation with violence of all kinds.

This beatitude calls us to be reconcilers, to advocate for peaceful resolutions of conflict, and to eschew violence of any kind. Nonviolent peacemakers protest in word and presence.

Yet in our present age, some professed Christians believe that taking out the bad guys with violence is justified. But America is riddled with violence and gun shootings of innocent children that are happening increasingly often. Armed and masked Immigration and Customs Enforcers on the streets of our cities makes America look more like a fascist country. Now in America if you are a migrant, a homeless person, or not a white person, you might well be grabbed and sent to a concentration camp–like jail.

Ann Coulter said, "We should invade their countries, kill their leaders, and convert them to Christianity. We weren't punctilious about locating and punishing only Hitler and his top officers. We carpet-bombed German cities; we killed civilians. That's war."[10] And Jerry Falwell said, "You've got to kill terrorists before the killing stops. And I'm for the President to chase them all over the world. If it takes ten years, blow them all away in the name of the Lord."[11]

9. Aptowicz, "Could You Stomach."

10. Quoted in Claiborne and Haw, *Jesus for President*, 177.

11. Quoted in Claiborne and Haw, *Jesus for President*, 177.

Not surprising are the rising numbers of post-traumatic stress symptoms and suicides among soldiers returning from violent wars in Vietnam, Afghanistan, Iraq, or other battlefields. In 2005 alone, there were 6,256 veteran suicides.[12] By 2023, gun violence in America had become an epidemic. Are Americans becoming immune to every new gun shooting in schools?

Embodied in the Greek and Hebrew definitions of peace, *eirene* and *shalom*, lies all that the word *blessed* means in the Beatitudes: happiness, well-being, contentment even. Jesus calls us to love our enemies, not to hold grudges, not even to be so angry and bitter that we fall into the temptation of murder, either by word or deed. Jesus elaborates on that in the rest of the Sermon on the Mount. He includes insults, slander, name-calling—the kind of angry words that demean and tear down another. Jesus tells us to turn the other cheek when someone strikes us. He asks us to forgive offenses seventy times seven. The only armor he advocates is the full armor of God: the belt of truth, the breastplate of righteousness, the shield of faith, the helmet of salvation, the sword of the Spirit, and the gospel of peace (Eph 6:13–17). The early Christians in the first four centuries were pacifists. So are most Anabaptists today.

My peacemaking actions first led me to Russia in 1989, to get to know my enemies, and kept me returning year after year. But peacemaking at home becomes more challenging, with close family members who, because of mental illness or addiction, have slandered and spoken evil against me. And not just family members, but also friends and colleagues have berated and accused me falsely. But my Christian faith has taught me not to hold grudges and not to allow my hurt to lead to resentment.

Peacemaking comes at great cost in any culture, particularly if one chooses not to serve in the military, to pray for enemies, to offer shelter and food to the homeless, and to minister to those in prison.

Ron Sider, speaking at a Mennonite World Conference in 1984, said of his denomination, which has a history and reputation of peacemaking, "Making peace is as costly as waging war. Unless

12. Claiborne and Haw, *Jesus for President*, 216.

we are prepared to pay the cost of peacemaking, we have no right to claim the label or preach the message."[13]

Jesus called peacemakers children of God. He said that our place in God's eternal dwelling will be assured, especially if we are persecuted or bullied here on Earth. Bullying, name-calling; physical, sexual, or emotional abuse—all cause untold damage to our human selves made in the image of God. If we have been so persecuted, let us with thankful hearts look forward to that time when we'll be fully initiated into God's domain.

BLESSED ARE THOSE WHO ARE PERSECUTED FOR RIGHTEOUSNESS' SAKE, FOR THEIRS IS THE KINGDOM OF GOD

According to Pastor Higgins, this eighth beatitude is a summary of all the others and is elaborated in the next verse:

> Blessed are you when people insult you and persecute you and say all kinds of evil things about you falsely on account of me. Rejoice and be glad, because your reward is great in heaven, for they persecuted the prophets before you in the same way. (Matt 5:11–12 NET)

One test of being in the age of Christ is to expect persecution. If one thinks being a Christian is all about being liked and admired, that's not what Jesus taught. Try living as a Christian in a Muslim country, or one where a hostile government lines up Christians in orange jumpsuits and chops off their heads for all the world to see.

13. Sider, "God's People Reconciling," para 40.

6

Jesus as the Way, the Truth, and the Life

JESUS AS THE WAY

***Pilgrims on the Way*, created by the author with Microsoft Copilot**

FIRST CENTURY CHRISTIANS WERE called the People of the Way because Thomas asked Jesus to tell him the way (John 14:6). Jesus responded that he was the Way and in doing so he used the term that God called himself, I AM.[1] Jesus called his way the narrower or more difficult way. He told his followers that the kin-dom of God was near when they healed the sick (Luke 10:9 NLT).

After Jesus' death and resurrection, when the apostles were sent out throughout Asia Minor, Italy, and Greece to preach and teach about Jesus, many who converted were slaves, but some were Greek-speaking citizens, some were Roman soldiers, and others were dignitaries in the Roman state. They preached the power and wisdom of the cross.

Looking for any leader who would save them from the tyranny of Rome, many who saw and heard Jesus speak in Galilee came to believe him to be their anticipated Messiah, the longed-for leader to rescue them from Roman occupation. Some of Jesus' disciples were thought to have Zealot sympathies, and Simon was a member of the radical Zealot party. After his resurrection, Jesus discouraged his disciples from this way of violence and taught them instead to continue following in his way—not the way of a conqueror but of a humble servant. If they believed and followed, they would do greater work than he did (John 14:12).

Meanwhile, Roman emperors were occupied in quelling rebellions and recruiting soldiers to fight and conquer. But as their rulers became more corrupt and power hungry, Christians were their scapegoats—the ones who caused all the problems.

But two centuries after Emperor Constantine signed a letter with Emperor Licinius that became the Edict of Milan, Christians were no longer persecuted. Christianity became the required religion of the empire. Devotion to following the way taught by Jesus diminished, and adherence to ecclesiastical hierarchy and dogma took precedent. People of the Way became people of the Roman Empire—the first incidence of the melding of church and state and a loss of the vibrancy of the Christian faith. In subsequent periods of Christian history, western and eastern Christians split into Roman Catholicism and Eastern Orthodoxy.

However, Christians didn't always follow Jesus' way. When Muslims took control of Holy Land territories and historical sites in

1. The Gospel of John has seven of Jesus' "I AM" statements.

the 600s, a hue and cry went out for knights in Catholic Europe to be raised up to lead armed troops to defeat the infidels. So, between AD 1095 and 1291, during the infamous period of the Great Crusades, following Jesus became synonymous with killing both Jews and Muslims. Thus began the persecution of anyone who wasn't a Christian, contrary to Jesus' teaching about loving your neighbor.

During medieval times in Europe and Spain, the Roman Catholic Church attempted to quell heresies. Protestants, Jews, and others were imprisoned, tortured, and put to death during the Inquisition in Spain. Even during the era of colonial America, some charismatic, clairvoyant Christian women were called witches and tortured.

When life grew too tough, groups of Christians in various periods of Christian history have lived in monasteries to lead ascetic lives to follow Jesus. In Russia, Christians who chose to follow Jesus were—and still are—called "Fools-for-Christ" (1 Cor 3:18–19), or those who follow a lifestyle of "holy insanity."[2] Saints days are named for them in the Russian Orthodox Church.

Pluralism, inclusiveness, or tolerance were three of the reasons that a convention in Baltimore that I attended deleted John 14:6. Most of the delegates to that convention believed that not leaving out that Bible passage in the resolution would turn off Jews, Muslims, and Sikhs. They were willing to compromise Jesus' message for the sake of not offending other religious traditions.

As early as AD 1470, Thomas à Kempis, a Dutch monk with the Brothers of the Common Life, who lived a life of poverty, chastity, and obedience, captured what it means to follow Jesus, writing the following:

> Follow me. I am the Way, the Truth and the Life. Without the Way, there is no going. Without the Truth, there is no knowing. Without the Life, there is no living. I am the Way which you must follow, the Truth which you must believe, the Life for which you must hope. I am the inviolable Way, the infallible Truth, the Life that is true, the blessed, the uncreated Life. If you abide in My Way

2. Orthodox Wiki, "Fool-for-Christ."

> you shall know the Truth, and the Truth shall make you free and you shall attain life everlasting.[3]

John Bunyan, writing in 1678, spoke of the tough road that Christians needed to take.[4]

God continues to beckon us to follow his son, Jesus, through the Holy Spirit, as this Holy Trinity icon symbolizes for us.

Icon of the Trinity by Andrei Rublev. Public domain.

3. Thomas à Kempis, *Imitation of Christ*, 124.
4. Bunyan, *Pilgrim's Progress*.

If you are a believer, you can meditate and pray with this icon. I've included a picture of it here for you to meditate on during your quiet time. You may turn away. Then turn back to gaze upon the Godhead again. As I look, I see three figures in unity with one another, separate yet bonded together in harmonious love for each other. They have angel wings. I'm reminded of the three angels who visited Abraham near the oak trees of Mamre. These three angels in the icon signify Jesus the Son, who sits at the Holy Table, God the Father, who gives Jesus his blessing, and the life-giving Holy Spirit, who looks out for me and points to my place at the Communion table.

Beckoning.

Inviting.

Seeming to imply: Sit with us and share in our union.

We hesitate to enter that narrow space, not sure about the suffering. The world beckons us to stay away, to say, "No thank you." We want to join others going into the more appealing space, a space that looks promising. Those others in the world laugh and seem to be having a good time. They hold out medicines to keep the pain away, tempting us to indulge in risky behaviors or games of chance that might earn us prestige and money, wealth and possessions, or enticing us to abuse alcohol and experiment with illegal drugs that might make us feel better.

If we seek to be followers of Jesus, we cannot have it both ways. We cannot serve God and Mammon or money, possessions, fame, status, or whatever is valued more than Jesus (Matt 6:24). Adhering to Jesus' way will inevitably lead to disobedience in adhering to cultural guidelines of our current age. In our present age, for example, wealth, fame, status, and power far too often take the place of what matters to God.

We gaze at the icon again. We want to leave. We are afraid. Political happenings and daily living distract our thoughts. We do want to contemplate the Holy Mystery. We feel guilty because our daily distractions and worldly concerns keep us from drawing closer. The good life promised by advertisements might give us temporary relief, temporary escape, and temporary glory.

Participating in Communion, we recognize our vulnerability, believing that Jesus can shield us from temptation, can do for us what we cannot do for ourselves. Others seek to withdraw from the world, to live in monastic communities so they can be less tempted, spending more structured time, according to the rule of the order, in prayer and meditation.

JESUS AS THE TRUTH

In America's culture absolute Truth, the truth we find in our digest of Scriptures, has been compromised. Few follow the Ten Commandments, Jesus' teachings, and our creeds. The qualities of sincerity and integrity, trustworthiness, and reality based on known knowledge have largely disappeared. Falsehoods and lies dominate.

When Pilate asked Jesus "What is truth?" (John 18:38 NIV), the question seemed relevant because many philosophies and mystery religions of that historical period professed different kinds of truths and pathways to Roman or Greek gods. Scholars debate about why Pilate asked Jesus that question. Jesus had just finished responding to Pilate about who he was and why he had come into the world: to bear witness to the truth. "Everyone who cares for truth, who has any feeling for the truth, recognizes my voice," Jesus responded. (John 18:37 MSG)

Perhaps Pilate was like many of my acquaintances who didn't understand what is involved in sending and going on a mission trip when they asked me the question, "When are you taking your next trip?" Maybe Pilate was a god-seeker, searching for something to believe in. Perhaps he was taking one of the popular philosophy classes of his day or attracted to one of the many mystery religions. If so, living with a variety of truths made sense, and he didn't honestly know which of the many truths to believe in. Maybe he was attracted to Jesus' sincerity and didn't really want an answer. Maybe the meeting had gone on longer than his schedule allowed and he needed to get on to the next case that would come before him. If any of my speculations are true, we don't know because the Bible doesn't tell us. We do know that he didn't wait for Jesus' response. Instead, he sent Jesus back to Jewish leaders to deal with him.

We have a Pilate issue today. Each of us has an opinion of what is truth, and each of us sees reality in a different way. We call our personal opinions objective or relative truth. Truth becomes distorted by adhering to political correctness, our own personality traits, what others insist that we believe, the dysfunction of our lives, or our acquiescence to another's concept of the truth; or, like Pilate, the truth doesn't matter that much to the way we conduct our lives. When a federal government accepts and perpetuates untruths, the whole country is damaged. Untruths underlie all mental pathology and personality disorders. In a popular television sitcom of the nineties called *Seinfeld*, the character George Costanza claimed that if you believe a lie, it becomes true.[5]

As Jesus followers, we need to be wary that we don't fall into the same trap. Just because many Americans believe that today we live in a post-Christian age, where anyone's version of the truth is as acceptable as another's, doesn't mean truth doesn't matter. "Alternate facts" claiming to be true are not.

Even different Christian traditions emphasize different truths. Far too often in Christian circles, we repeat false and half-truths as if they are the whole truth. Here are some of the more popular ones:

- If you accept Jesus as your Lord and Savior, you are saved and can do no wrong.
- If you follow Jesus, you will be blessed with prosperity and good fortune.
- If you do good works here on earth, you will be rewarded in the next life.
- Money is the root of all evil.
- Whatever happens is in God's plan. Keep your chin up; he won't give you more than you can handle.
- God helps those who help themselves.

5. Seinfeldism.com, "S06E16."

- Everything in the Bible is literally true.
- We are in a spiritual battle to conquer the evil world for Christ.

The Bible does hold truth and honesty to be important. From Genesis through Deuteronomy and the books of the New Testament, one can find 139 references to truth. In Genesis, several passages speak of offering proof of the truth of a statement. The prophet Jeremiah laments that false prophets commit adultery, are dishonest, and set an example for others to follow (Jer 23:14). Proverbs 23 emphasizes the importance of truth to be wise and understanding. Isaiah (10) decries rebellious people who tell lies and don't want to do what is right. In Paul's letter to the Romans, he warns against the wicked and godless men who suppress the truth by their wickedness; they became fools and exchange the glory of God for despicable behavior with each other. "They exchanged the truth of God for a lie, and worshipped and served the creature rather than the Creator" (Rom 1:25 ASV).

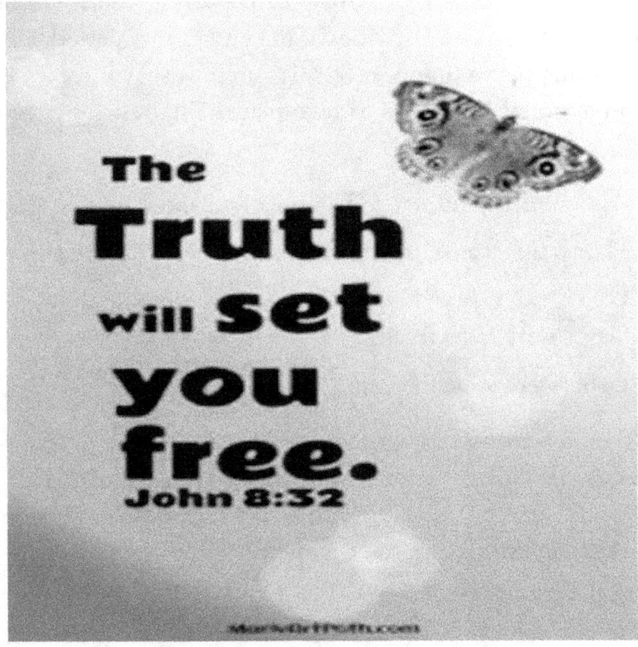

Created by Marivic Barrios. Used with permission.

Make a copy. Hang this on your door handle. Glue it to your mirror or post it near your computer. Get out your Bible. Read it daily. Inwardly digest what it says. Live the Jesus way.

To whet your appetite and set you on your course, let's move on to the last part of how Jesus wants us to live.

JESUS AS THE LIFE

When Jesus read the passage from Isaiah that announced the Year of the Jubilee, he proclaimed that he is the fulfillment of Isaiah's promise and that the time of Jubilee had come, introducing the inbreaking of the age of Christ. His listeners—folks worshiping that day in the synagogue—did not want to lose their livelihood if this was to be the Year of the Jubilee. Maybe that was another reason they tried to push him off a cliff!

The Year of the Jubilee was an Old Testament practice at the end of a seven-times-seven-year period in the Hebrew calendar.[6] A special ram's horn was blown on the Day of Atonement to signal the start of the Jubilee festivities at the end of that period. During the following year, a time of reversal from the usual practices of the economic life of Israel was to take place. Three social-economic activities ceased:

- Agricultural land was to lie unplanted and unharvested.
- Plants that came up by themselves were for the poor to harvest.
- Slaves were to be freed.
- Debts were to be forgiven.

God's requirements, as written in Exodus, Deuteronomy, and Leviticus, included the provision of the fiftieth year after the forty-ninth year for restoring land ownership to the original owners—really upsetting the socioeconomic order. In that period of Israel's history under Roman rule, many were enslaved because

6. Kraybill, *Upside-Down Kingdom*, 98.

they couldn't pay their debts. The wealthy, mainly the Pharisees and landowners, were becoming richer—like what is happening in this country where the 1% benefit, the middle class disappears, and the poor carry the brunt of the burden of our society. Imagine the outcry if Wall Street had to lay inactive for a year and our tax laws favored the poor!

Establishing Jubilee life may sound like socialism to some, yet the Jubilee Year was based on the idea that the sixth year in every seven-year cycle would be a year of plenty so that the Israelites could prepare to let the land lay fallow at the end of the forty-ninth year. In fact, one of the principles of good farming is to rotate crops, allowing some fields to lie fallow, not necessarily every seventh of seven years, but the idea is the same. However, even then, when Jesus proposed that the principles of the Jubilee would be realized in the age of Christ, the idea was a radical revolutionary concept; good news to the poor but bad news to the wealthy and those who wanted their debts to be paid back. Think of our bankruptcy laws; they seem to embody one aspect of the Jubilee concept. Or think of prison fellowship ministries, or feeding the hungry, or welcoming immigrants. These American Christian ministries are at the forefront of showing us what the age of the Christian church is like.

Life in the age of the church challenges most of us daily because, even though Jesus conquered death and sin on the cross, we still live together as Christians in faith communities, where redeemed sinners gather to receive God's grace.

7

Citizenship in God's Domain

THE INVITATION

Jesus invites everyone to become citizens, the same invitation Jesus gave to his first disciples. Remember when he called the fishermen James and his brother John, sons of Zebedee? The two brothers left their father and the fishing business to follow him. Jesus asks some of his followers today to leave businesses and professions; others, he just asks to spend more time with him. That may mean instead of getting ahead in our jobs or earning more money, the focus will be on trying to live the way he wants us to live; to love God and our neighbors as we love ourselves (Luke 10:27).

In one of his parables, Jesus talked about his invitation to attend a heavenly banquet (Matt 22:1–14). There were two invitations sent: the first, like our "Save the Date" cards, and then the more formal invitation. The last invitation was closer to the actual time, and said, *Come, the feast is on the table.*

All who received the official invitations refused or had excuses as to why they couldn't attend. One may have had a business appointment. Another may have had to attend a funeral. Another might not have had the right clothes. When all invitees either couldn't come or replied that they would come late, the host—meaning Jesus—went out into the streets and invited others, presumably outcasts, the homeless, women (maybe even some prostitutes), prisoners, and immigrants (maybe Roman soldiers or slaves)—people looked down upon by the religious establishment.

***Heavenly Banquet Table*, created by the author with Microsoft Copilot**

Jesus might say to all of us, *Here I am. I'm inviting you to step into the blessings God has for you. All you have to do is say you believe and follow me.*

Accepting this invitation also requires that the first shall be last and the last first. Jesus teaches this in several places, once earlier in Luke's gospel having to do with the seating at the banquet:

> When you are invited, go and take the least important place, so that when your host approaches, he will say to you, "Friend, move up here to a better place." Then you will be honored in the presence of all who share the

> meal with you. For everyone who exalts himself will be humbled, but the one who humbles himself will be exalted. (Luke 14:10–11 NET)

Another time, when James and John were vying for who would sit beside Jesus in his realm, Jesus said,

> You know that the rulers of the Gentiles lord it over them, and those in high positions use their authority over them. It must not be this way among you! Instead, whoever wants to be great among you must be your servant, and whoever wants to be first among you must be your slave. (Matt 20:25–27 NIV)

Once a seminary professor and his wife came to visit my husband and me at our lake vacation home along with several other couples. In that house, we had two guest rooms and a loft over our living area. The best guest room we offered to our guests, but the professor and his wife chose the loft, where they had to climb stairs and be exposed to the whole living area. When they chose this less desirable location to sleep, we thought of the less desirable place where Jesus was born, in the ground-floor room with the animals.

A woman living at a shelter for women across the street from our downtown church attended a morning prayer service with a group of us. After attending for several weeks, her familiarity with both the prayers and the Bible readings so impressed us I invited her to attend a home Bible study fellowship one evening. The next morning the hostess called the church office, complaining that I had brought "that smelly woman."

Which woman would be welcome as a citizen in God's dwelling: the woman who hosted the Bible study or the homeless woman?

Donald Kraybill calls followers of Jesus who have now accepted his invitation to come to the banquet to prepare themselves by living differently than the way their culture and society lives, including church-going folks, no matter what period of history. "Jesus has just turned our social worlds upside down."[1]

1. Kraybill, *Upside-Down Kingdom*, 275.

PARABLES: STORIES DESCRIBED

Through his parables Jesus showed his followers how to live in God's domain on earth. Many books have been written analyzing Jesus' parables. In Perkins's book *Hearing the Parables of Jesus*, you will find a few to help understand the setting and circumstances of the stories Jesus told. Storytelling was the best way Jesus' followers could remember his teachings. Those who listened may have been illiterate. Most learned their own history through lessons passed on in each generation to the next generation. One could spend hours following and listening to itinerant preachers and teachers. However, Jesus warned that many of them were false prophets.

Some days Jesus must have been discouraged about whether his followers understood his message about life in the age of Christ. On one occasion he told his disciples,

> This is why I use these stories to teach the people: They see, but they don't really see. They hear, but they don't really hear or understand. So, they show that what Isaiah said about them is true: "You people will listen and listen, but you will not understand. You will look and look, but you will not really see. Yes, the minds of these people are now closed. They have ears, but they don't listen. They have eyes, but they refuse to see. If their minds were not closed, they might see with their eyes; they might hear with their ears; they might understand with their minds. Then they might turn back to me and be healed." (Matt 13:13–15 ERV)

Sometimes Jesus used ordinary imagery, such as salt and light, to make a point. He taught his followers to be the salt of the earth. Salt was indeed a precious commodity for preserving and flavoring foods. His listeners knew that salt had real value in their daily lives. Paul referred to salt as wisdom and knowledge (Col 4:6).

Have you ever had a cup of chicken noodle soup that had no flavor, that needed salt to make it palatable? For those of us who follow Jesus, we need to keep our saltiness. Hans-Ruedi Weber,[2]

2. Weber, *Salty Christians*.

speaks of the people of God who follow Jesus as being a peculiar people, a missionary people who are in the world but not of the world, living as human beings in their worldly lives, but at the same time being holy.

Jesus encourages us Christians not to hide our lights under a bushel; instead, we must witness to Christ in the way we lead our lives so that when people see our good works, they will glorify God. This contrasts with those who boast of their good deeds for their own self-adulation.

Angry words, bullying, put-downs, adultery, lust—that includes sexual harassment—all these Jesus condemns. Most important of all, Jesus condemns revenge. Instead, he asks us to love our enemies and to resist with nonviolence.

The story of *Les Misérables* by Victor Hugo epitomizes the essence of the gospel message of that kind of love. As you may recall, Jean Valjean escaped from prison to a church for refuge. After accepting the bishop's hospitality and food, he stole the silver flatware during the night and took off. The local police rearrested him and returned the silver with Jean Valjean in handcuffs. The bishop told the policeman that he had given him the silver as a gift, handing him the silver candlesticks as well. Then the bishop blessed Jean Valjean by telling him that he needed to give up evil and espouse good. Jean Valjean then does much good with the rest of his life, raising a dying prostitute's child and offering employment to many.

Think about the parable or story of the mustard seed (Matt 13:30–32). Mustard bushes were like weeds that grew along fields and byways, like dandelions. Yet, the bush's seed was the smallest of all seeds. In fact, in several stories, Jesus used sowing seeds to illustrate growing under his leadership.

Seed Planting, by Tamera Teets. Used with permission.

When a sower scatters even a grain of mustard seed on the ground, it grows into a plant the size of a great shrub with large branches, like the planting of Jesus' kin-dom. What Jesus planted has grown into 2.6 billion Christians in the world today.[3] Today, even a Christian's smallest acts of kindness, forgiveness, mercy, and peacemaking are seeds that will keep the kin-dom growing.

Or consider the story of the rich man and Lazarus (Luke 16:19–31). This story describes wealthy men and women of any period who dress in the most expensive, latest-style clothing, eating gourmet food every day, their every whim pampered, with several expensive homes and money spent on themselves. In contrast, Lazarus, the beggar in the story, was like the poor with us today. Lazarus may be someone who holds down two jobs to feed their family and who can't afford to purchase a home. Lazarus may be an elderly widow or widower living on social security who must choose between eating, paying the rent, or paying for medicines. The very poor, like Lazarus, could be the ones who live on the streets or in shelters or those who depend on Medicaid to take care of their health needs. The very poor are in places where the homeless and the destitute rummage through garbage cans and dumpsters for leftover food from a wealthy man's table. Their

3. Zurlo, "World Christianity."

health needs—in the way of sores—have not received any attention, because they can't afford insurance.

***Rich Man and Beggar*, by Tamera Teets. Used with permission.**

When each dies, the wealthy go to Hades and the poor go to heaven or "paradise," to be with God. When the wealthy, now in torment, appeal to God for mercy they receive no grace. Still pleading, the wealthy ask God if they can go back to warn relatives still alive, warning them to change their lifestyles so they won't be in torment too when they die. God doesn't offer much hope for those relatives, who may be accumulating more money and goods while making as much profit as possible in the stock market.

The wealthy in the biblical story lack mercy because they see nothing wrong with their lifestyle; in fact, they believe they are entitled to their riches—as do the titans of social media companies. As for the poor in America—they have to choose to purchase health insurance or buy food. Wealthy Americans say, *God helps those who help themselves*. But that's not the way it is in God's plan.

8

Challenges: Eschatology Theories and Christian Heresies

DURING THE LAST FEW centuries, Christians have been concerned about when Jesus would return. During the first centuries of Christianity, Christians led their lives as best they could, anticipating that Jesus would return soon. Sometimes during wars, famines, and earthquakes followers of Jesus thought he would return soon. When the first thousand years ended and the time came to turn the calendar to day one of the year two thousand, some gathered to wait for Jesus, having sold their worldly possessions, but when the calendar turned, life went on as before.

"Eschatology" means the study of the end times in God's plan. The eschaton is the time between Jesus' time on earth and his second coming back to earth to usher in a new heaven and a new earth. God initiated his plan by first sending his son, Jesus, to teach and live the ways of God's domain and to die to redeem us from sin and be resurrected. Then, Jesus sent the Holy Spirit to be our comforter and guide for the interim time, called "inaugurated" or "realized" eschatology or the Age of the Church, to exist until Jesus will return. At that time, he will come to judge the quick and the dead and we will be forever in Jesus' fellowship. The first century Christians, including his loyal followers, believed he would return any day, even though he told them that he did not even know when the time of his return would be.

> But of that day or that hour no one knows, not even the angels in heaven, nor the Son, but only the Father. Take heed, watch; for you do not know when the time will come. It is like a man going on a journey, when he leaves home and puts his servants in charge, each with his work, and commands the doorkeeper to be on the watch. (Mark 13:32–34 NIV)

Church denominations and even individual Christians hold different eschatological concepts centered around the millennial period (Rev 10 and 1 Thess 4) to explain the in-between time:

- *Amillennialism* means the thousand-year millennium time was inaugurated by Jesus, who taught about and ushered in the domain of God. Since his death and resurrection, Jesus is always present to intercede for us, his believers.[1]
- *Premillennialism* theorizes that Jesus will come back to earth after a period of tribulation. Then, Jesus will reign during a millennium period of peace and prosperity.
- *Dispensationalism* is a form of premillennialism that includes the rapture, before a period of tribulation and before the millennium when Jesus will begin his reign.
- *Postmillennialism* speculates that Jesus will not return until after a millennium golden age where everyone has been saved and living in a time of peace and prosperity.

When these eschatological theories surfaced in theological discussions in the nineteenth and twentieth centuries—having not been considered important in the preceding years—various millennium theories developed, according to my former Anglican bishop/professor of systematic theology, John Rodgers. Dr. Rodgers described four final events considered important to all these theories:

1. Rodgers, *Essential Truths for Christians*, 138.

1. The second coming of Jesus.
2. The resurrection of the dead.
3. The final judgment of man.
4. The final states of heaven and hell.

Nowhere is the rapture mentioned.[2]

More important than theories of the second coming and the end times is whether we follow and know Jesus today and tomorrow, based on what he teaches us in his spoken words as recorded in the New Testament, and whether we will be ready and prepared when he does return.

Along with speculation about when Jesus will return and various millennial theories, Christianity has been plagued with heretical beliefs at various times when church bishops (who are commissioned to keep the faith once given to the disciples) held ecumenical councils to clarify what they confirmed to be true, what was speculation, and what was false.

There have been many heresies. Here are a few of the more dangerous ones:

- *Gnosticism* (appeared in AD 140): The material world is evil. Salvation comes through secret knowledge.
- *Montanism* (AD 157): Prophetic ecstasy is important.
- *Manichaeism* (fourth century): The material world is evil. The spirit world is good.
- *Docetism*: Jesus appeared human but really wasn't human.
- *Arianism*: Jesus was created by God but was not eternal or a member of the godhead.
- *Monarchianism*: The Father, Son, and Holy Spirit are not one.
- *Pelagianism*: Original sin did not impact human nature. Man's will is still capable of choosing good.

2. Rodgers, *Essential Truths for Christians*, 139–41.

With its prolific number of styles of Christianity in the United States, Americans are prone to become attracted to some of these heretical beliefs and eschatological concepts. Before exploring two, Christian nationalism and Zionism, becoming familiar with their meanings will be important.

However, exploring periods of church history when the rulers of the state attempted to mold people into its version of Christianity and times when the leaders of the Christian church decided the fate of the state will both be necessary, especially when violence, hatred, or greed were prevalent. God doesn't like these options. The travails of church and state have proven repeatedly in church history that when the human sins of intolerance, power, greed, racism, prejudice, and superiority take over, Jesus suffers. When Christian nations use violence against Jews or Muslims or against those Christians who believe differently, God cries. During those times, what Jesus taught his disciples and passed on throughout the ages about how to be Christian citizens gets lost. He sighs and turns away when we miss the mark on what it means to be his followers.

Let's return to the old Roman Empire first.

PART III

Church and State

9

Constantine and the Cross

THE ROMAN EMPIRE EVENTUALLY became more tolerant of Christ followers beginning in AD 312. That year Emperor Constantine either had a vision of the cross in a battle or had a dream about seeing the cross. In either case, he came to believe that the cross was the sign that he would conquer in battle. Another theory conjectured that Constantine had his soldiers paint crosses on their shields.[1] Whatever happened, along with his victory in battle, the cross became equated with a sign of his religious piety.

In AD 313, Emperor Constantine signed the Edict of Milan, granting tolerance for all religions in the Empire, including Christianity. Eventually, Constantine became the patron of Christians, built churches, and ordered Bibles copied. Those who didn't convert were required to pay for building churches.

Constantine claimed to have a special and personal relationship with the Christian God, but he wasn't baptized until on his death bed. Instead, he continued his military conquests even though most of Jesus' followers at that period were pacifists. According to the culture in both Greece and Rome, military success and religious piety went together.

Constantine's mother, Helena, took a pilgrimage to the Holy Land and was thus deemed by the church to be a saint. Yet, whether

1. Rodney, "Constantine's Vision," para. 7.

her son Constantine's conversion led to becoming more like Jesus is in question, because he reputedly became more ruthless after his conversion.[2]

Under Constantine's rule as emperor, the church first became entwined with the state. He had a divine right, appointing bishops who had dual roles of being overseers in the church and ambassadors for the state. Under his rule, he took on quelling Christian heresies and setting up ecumenical councils to deal with them. At one point, Emperor Constantine called himself "a bishop outside the church."[3]

Eventually Christianity split into two camps; one in the west (in Rome, known as the Western church) and one in the east (in Constantinople, known as the Eastern Orthodox Church). From then on, Orthodox churches identified themselves with a country and some became an instrument of that country's politics.

Throughout Christian history, both western and eastern church officials have become more like ruthless autocrats—power hungry, money-grabbing demigods. At other times, the state leader has controlled both state and church, such as the kings in England or Spain, or the church leader has controlled both church and state, as happened with Roman Catholic church officials in the first few centuries after Constantine.

The collusion of the leaders of both church and state, as will be explored in a later section, far too often creates problems for both institutions. Martin Luther called church and state issues the doctrine of two kingdoms.[4] Either kingdom can lead the other astray. One can have a positive or negative impact on the other.

2. Matthews et al., "Constantine I," sec. "Legacy of Constantine I."

3. Matthews, "Constantine I."

4. Altman, "Interpreting the Doctrine."

10

Reformation Occurs

ONCE THE ROMAN EMPIRE adopted Christianity as the state religion, the governments they established throughout the conquered Gaelic territories became weaker. Roman popes, along with their bishops and clerics—holding both spiritual and secular power for centuries—eventually led to corruption in the church. Not only the pope's supremacy but also the entire hierarchical structure and its power over the people grew increasingly alarming. By the 1600s it was as if the Roman Catholic Church ruled the world.

When repentant sinners entered the confessional to receive absolution or forgiveness of their sin from a priest, that was not the end. Depending upon the sin that the repentant person committed, they still needed to do acts of atonement, partial or plenary, depending on the severity of the sin or sins committed. Priests and bishops set up a system of indulgences, or gifts of God's grace. During the Middle Ages, the givers of that grace were involved in immoral and sinful acts themselves. Yet, they even had the audacity to sell indulgences. While they became wealthy, their sins abounded, and the repentant sinner became poorer.

This injustice continued until one monastic scholar named Martin Luther not only protested but also acted to raise awareness. In AD 1505, he joined an Augustinian monastic community, where he studied Catholic theology with a concentration on indulgences. Then, he was given a professorship at Wittenberg

University—considered a radical university at that time—where he posted ninety-five theses on the door of the Castle Church protesting indulgences. That action drew the attention of the Catholic hierarchy who called him before the Edict of Worms, declared him a heretic, and excommunicated him.[1]

Meanwhile, thanks to the invention of the printing press, his ninety-five theses against indulgences were printed and widely disseminated. Since Martin Luther also had an opportunity to read and then teach from Paul's Epistle to the Romans, his teaching that salvation comes from God's grace alone was also widely printed and circulated. He even translated the Bible into German so that anyone could now read the biblical texts for themselves.

The priesthood of believers—rather than a priesthood of clerics only—came to define the church. Many Protestant denominations resulted: Lutherans, Baptists, Puritans, Anabaptists, Anglicans, and Presbyterians. The Moravian Church had already been established.

Now the ruler of the secular government either supported the demise of authoritarianism under the clerics of the Roman Church and maneuvered their way around competing Protestant and Catholic churches, or the prevailing denomination—such as the Anabaptists in Switzerland or Anglicans in England—became the state religion.

1. Paraphrase from Hillerbrand, "Martin Luther."

PART IV

Troubling Examples

11

Nazi Germany and One Church

Fast forward to the twentieth century to examine what happens to both church and state when a dictator comes to power.[1]

Before World War I, Germany had been a dynamic industrial nation with military might. The Protestant Church Federation—Lutherans, Reformed, and United churches—Roman Catholics, and free churches flourished. That changed when Hitler came into power.

Adolf Hitler was the oldest son of Alois, a harsh disciplinarian whom Adolf feared and disliked. His father sent Adolf to be educated at a nearby Benedictine monastery. There, Adolf dreamed of greatness but was lazy and bad-tempered. After graduating, he lived a bohemian existence, staying in flophouses while working as an artist. But he joined the German Army during WWI, where he rose to the position of corporal. When gassed in the trenches, he received the Iron Cross for bravery and became a recluse.

In 1920, a new Nationalsozialistisch Deutsche Arbeiterpartei (Nazi) party attracted his attention. Hitler became its chief propagandist. The newly formed Nazi party espoused a kind of national socialism with the battle cry of "Rise up German Aryans and be mighty once again." Adolf Hitler's ability to organize and fundraise

1. The summary that follows is based on Kaufman, *Rise and Fall,* and a paper entitled "Let's Learn Lessons from 1930s Germany" presented by John S. Weber at a conference I attended in 2016.

plus his charismatic personality drew huge crowds to his rallies. He attempted a coup to take over the party but instead was arrested and sentenced to five years in prison, though he only served nine months due to his popularity. By then the members of the party were caught up in his cult of personality and purchased his book, *Mein Kampf*, which he wrote while in prison to define his vision of a fascist state.

Meanwhile violence had increased in the streets and communism was capturing the attention of the German people.

When Adolf was released from prison, he continued to hold rallies, capturing the crowds with his charisma, a new Nazi flag, and a new national salute, *Heil Hitler.* Hitler renamed his storm troopers, whom he had earlier trained to restore law and order, the SA (*Sturmabteilung*), which later became the SS (*Schutzstaffel*). When Hitler became head of the Nazi party there were twenty times more SA than in the German Army.

During this period, Hitler's mentor was Dietrich Eckart, who taught him to love the music of Richard Wagner, a notorious anti-Semite. The Ring Cycle, the name of Wagner's operas, were written based on Amalek, a descendant of Esau, whose birthright blessing was destroyed by Jacob. Amalek wanted to destroy the Jewish people (Exod 17:8).

Hitler was also friendly with the Arab leader Al Jazeera, who also hated Jews and used the Nazi salute. According to Hitler's autobiography, *Mein Kampf*, "Rational anti-Semitism must lead to systematic legal opposition. Its final objective must be the removal of the Jews altogether." In *Mein Kampf*, he described the Jew as the "destroyer of culture," "a parasite within the nation," and "a menace."[2]

Erik Larson quotes from Christopher Isherwood in his *Berlin Stories* about Hitler's attraction as follows: "Hitler is the master of this city (Berlin). The sun shines, and dozens of my friends . . . are in prison, possibly dead."[3] His storm troopers arrested, beat, and murdered communists, socialists, and Jews.

2. Knapp et al., "Adolf Hitler," para. 6.

3. Larson, *In the Garden*, 56.

By 1932, the Nazi party had won over most of the electorate. Hitler convinced the industrial barons to support him so that he could run for president. While the Weimar Republic continued to crumble, their political leaders made a deal with Hitler so that he could become chancellor. His first action was to destroy the parliament, while his gestapo rounded up any opposition. The Third Reich was born and the persecution of German Jews continued with zeal.

By the spring of 1934, Martha Roberts, the daughter of the American ambassador William Dodds, wrote,

> What I had heard, seen and felt, revealed to me that the conditions of living were worse than in pre-Hitler days, that the most complicated and heartbreaking system of terror ruled the country, repressed the freedom and happiness of the people, and German leaders were inevitably leading these docile and kindly masses into another war.[4]

Hitler's stature grew so that by 1936 he was godlike. He told the German people, "That you have found me . . . among so many millions is the miracle of our time! And that I have found you, that is Germany's fortune!"[5]

One of the Führer's strategies as chancellor was to coordinate all aspects of society. Consolidation of all the Protestant denominations and churches came first. He heartily supported a German Christian movement, a group of Protestants who wanted the Christian churches to include only true Germans, thus excluding anyone from Jewish descent. In 1933, all regional churches, including Roman Catholics, became one national church, with a Nazi party member, Ludwig Müller, as bishop.

Many Germans embraced this National Christian Movement whose mission and battle cry, "One Nation! One God! One Reich! One Church!" resounded from pulpits and pews.[6] Some even called themselves "Storm Troopers for Christ." Combining

4. Larson, *In the Garden*, loc. 4513.
5. Quoted in Wikipedia, "Adolf Hitler's," sec. "Religious aspects," para. 2.
6. Facing History and Ourselves, "Protestant Churches," para. 3.

church and state in this way, German Christians embraced Nazi anti-Semitism, proclaiming that only Aryan Germans—with no Jewish blood—were Christians. They also excluded anyone with any physical or mental deformity in order to create a "pure" spiritual Third Reich homeland.

Whether the Nazi party co-opted the German Protestants and Roman Catholics or whether Aryan German Christians were just trying to survive remains for history to decide. But when Hitler and his storm troopers first identified and isolated Jews in ghettos, the German gestapo or storm troopers rounded them up and sent them to concentration camps. Most were exterminated. Six million Jews died in what today we call the Holocaust, and sixty to eighty million people from England, Europe, the Soviet Union, and America died fighting.

Unfortunately, America and its allies far too often tried to be nice and appease Hitler. A professor of strategic studies at the British National Defense University even convinced the British government to make a deal for Hitler to take over the territory of Czechoslovakia.[7]

7. Novo, "Ukraine and the Lessons."

12

Russian Marriage of Church and State

RUSSIANS AND RUSSIAN ORTHODOXY

THE RUSSIANS' DEVOTION TO their Russian Orthodox faith originated in the medieval kingdom of Kievan Rus' in AD 988 when Prince Vladimir was baptized in the Dnieper River in what was then the Rus Empire. Vladimir, like the Roman Emperor Constantine who supported the creation of popes in the Roman Catholic Church, made Orthodox Christianity the official religion of his kingdom. Since that time, Christianity has had a profound influence on the history of both Russia and Ukraine.

For more than 1,450 years, first under the princes, then under the shahs and khans of the Mongols, then under the tsars, the Russian people knew only a centralized form of government and the Orthodox brand of Christianity.

The Communist Revolution, as a reaction to the wealth and indulgences of the established Orthodox Church and tsar, espoused atheism and tried to do away with all religions. Stalin attempted to liquidate both religion and morality in the Soviet Union. Then, Soviet Russia devoured and enslaved all its neighboring nations.

Anatoly Lunacharsky, the commissar for education in 1933, stated that Christians must be considered the worst of enemies.[1]

1. Hill, *Puzzle of the Soviet*, 2.

The Soviet regime took the lives of forty-two thousand priests and closed five hundred of the six hundred churches in Moscow alone. By 1941, ninety-eight out of every one hundred Orthodox churches no longer existed. The government had either destroyed church buildings or turned them into museums and factories. Although some Protestant sects, primarily Baptist, Lutheran, Armenian Apostolic, and Methodist, coexisted with the Russian Orthodox Church, many evangelical leaders were shipped off to Siberia to slow death by starvation and torture.[2]

My first experience of Russia—then the former Soviet Union—was in 1989 when I joined a Peace Odyssey trip to meet and build bridges with the Russian people during the height of the Cold War.

The year before I took my first trip marked the one-thousand-year anniversary of the formal baptism of the Eastern Slavs into Byzantine Christianity. Prince Vladimir, moved by the beauty and mystery of the Orthodox worship service when he visited Constantinople, converted to that faith.

During our Odyssey trip the golden spires of the Church of Our Savior, one of the cherished Russian churches demolished by the Soviets to become a public swimming pool, once again rose above the Moscow skyline.

On a later trip, I stood before another commemorative memorial in Kiev, Ukraine, while the battle for the birthplace of Russian Orthodoxy smoldered.

During the 1990s, Soviet citizens flocked to be baptized, to read the Bible, and to learn all they could about Christianity. Thanks to an influx of evangelists and church planters, with their message of redemption, justice, and peace, house churches became worshiping congregations and leased space to worship or acquired buildings.

2. Hill, *Puzzle of the Soviet*, 116.

Photo of the author in Moscow

My missionary friend, Pam Brunson, called me in 1996 and asked for help in facilitating a seminar on alcohol addiction, treatment, and prevention. Under the Soviet regime, bosses used to pay employees in Vodka, so alcoholism was a huge problem. In September of 1997, a group of us—all professionals—journeyed to Moscow to facilitate that training, the first of many trainings that followed.[3]

Russian Orthodox Church leaders criticized the new churches being planted and were suspicious of the recovery rehab programs we introduced. Fortunately, one of the attendees at our workshop in 1977, Katya Savina, a devout Russian Orthodox believer, proved

3. Webb, *Memories and Miracles*.

them wrong by starting her own rehabilitation center called Zebra. In time, she convinced Orthodox church believers of the legitimacy of the recovery process, and the newly emerging government supported her program until Vladimir Putin was elected president.

Then, patriarch Alexy II, concerned about the growth of new evangelical churches, pushed through the duma a new law: the Law on Freedom of Conscience and Religious Associations. Under that law, religious associations not registered since 1982 needed to register every fifteen years, and only Russians would have the right to form these new associations.

ORTHODOXY AND PUTIN ENTWINED

Vladimir Putin was born in Leningrad to parents who worked in the local factory. His mother probably named her son Vladimir after the famous Rus prince and, reputedly, had him secretly baptized in one of the hidden forest services. Vladimir became known in his youth as a street fighter, probably encountering and killing many rats living in and near their communal communist style apartment building. His career path, as was customary, was chosen for him by the Communist party. He studied law and became fluent in the German language; then, he joined the KGB as an agent, eventually assigned to serve in that intelligence agency in East Germany. He was asked to join the Yeltsin administration in 1996 as director of the newly formed FSB, or security administration. Finally, he was elected prime minister in 1999, while I was still going back and forth to cities in the newly formed Russian Federation.

On my many mission training trips, I watched and listened to old timers who gathered in the streets, crying out for a restoration of life during the time of the tsars. Businessmen whom I met had set up kiosks to sell goods, while professionals praised Putin for stabilizing a tottering Russian economy.

In his role as prime minister, Putin courted the new oligarchs of the oil and gas industry who had acquired their wealth with the help of oil men from Texas. I met several of them on an Aeroflot flight from Moscow to Novgorod in 1999. Putin also established relationships with both Patriarchs Alexy and Kirill, so that when he was elected president in 2012, church and state became synchronized. Those who had gathered in the woods to worship could now come out of hiding.

In 2017, Putin approved a package of laws restricting missionary activity and evangelism. These laws included ones that determined that one would not be allowed to share one's faith in homes, online, or anywhere else except church buildings. Around the same time, even Katya's Zebra rehabilitation program lost its government endorsement.

Putin's dictatorial rule of Russia includes restoring the Slavic territory in Europe back to that of the old Rus Empire. Remember that elderly Russians wanted to bring back the days of the tsars, who created the old Rus Empire. Now Patriarch Kirill supported and encouraged the invasion of Ukraine because he needed to bring the Orthodox Christians in Ukraine back into the Russian fold. After all, he also remembered that Ukraine and Belarus had both been part of that empire. But first Putin needed to reclaim the Crimean Peninsula for strategic access to the Black Sea, another reason for invading Ukraine.

13

The War of the Fiefdoms in Britain

In AD 597, the Roman Pope Gregory sent Augustine of Can with a missionary team to convert the Anglo Saxons and Celts on the island of Britannia. At that time there were many different small kingdoms. But Christianity grew rapidly, and church bishops became wealthy property owners.

However, in the Middle Ages conflicts between the church and the ruling monarch occurred over who had more authority. While Henry II reigned, he had the Archbishop Thomas Becket killed.

Finally, the reigning monarch became the ultimate authority in Britain in the sixteenth century. Henry VIII wanted to divorce his first wife and marry Anne Boleyn, but the current pope said no. That made the king so angry he decided to form his own church, calling it the Church of England or the Anglican Church, with himself as head. At that time the Benedictine monasteries were flourishing. Henry VIII took over those too, acquiring their wealth and properties.

Since this was also the period of the Reformation, the Anglican Church, with its catholic liturgy and sacraments, became Protestant. But Protestantism on the island of Britannia—known now as Great Britain—was split between Celtic worship in Ireland and Anglican worship in England. Up until the time of Queen Mary, Roman Catholics were tolerated or persecuted depending on the whim of the royalty in charge. As soon as Mary became queen she was known as Bloody Mary because she took her wrath out on the Protestants.

In 1534, under the reign of Queen Elizabeth, an Act of Supremacy was passed making the reigning royalty officially supreme governor of the Church of England. The queen then appointed the archbishop of Canterbury as head of the Church of England.

However, over the centuries, as the monarchy changed hands, either Roman Catholics or Protestants were persecuted and/or killed depending on which the reigning monarch chose as their denomination of choice. This resulted in the war of the fiefdoms, known as the British Civil Wars or the wars of the kingdoms. Sometimes the war was territorial, between the English and the Scots or the English and the Welsh,[1] or religious, such as the battle in Northern Ireland between the Protestants who wanted to be part of England and the Catholics who wanted to be separate.

Learning how the English Puritans—called "Puritans" because they wanted the Anglican Church to be less Catholic in its worship and trappings and more focused on piety—fared under the wars of the fiefdoms is important in understanding American history. When Anglicanism became the officially recognized Church of England, Puritans were forced out by Henry VIII. When restored in 1620, they gathered in what were called Nonconformist denominations.[2] About twenty thousand of them immigrated to New England between the 1620s and 1640s, establishing the Massachusetts Bay Colony, escaping the tyrannical reign of King Charles, who ruled as an absolute authoritarian monarch—that included control of the Church of England—claiming he had a divine right to make decisions without parliament.

1. Wikipedia, "History of the Church."
2. Wikipedia, "Wars of the Three."

PART V

Church and State in America

14

America's Experiment and Experience

AMERICA BEGAN WHEN DEVOUT English Puritans wanted to worship God in freedom from both their authoritarian monarch and the Catholic ritualism of the Church of England. Following the first settlement, the Massachusetts Bay Company sponsored another group of what we now call pilgrims. One thousand Puritans followed the first immigrants ten years later. This second wave of immigrants established the first all-English colony in Jamestown, Virginia. Both groups remained subjects of the King of England until the American Revolution and the Declaration of Independence in 1776. During the American Revolution, sentiments were divided between loyalty to the King of England and those who wanted to be separate.

The slave trade was introduced as early as 1493 when Christopher Columbus was sent by European imperialists to "discover" America for a new promised land for Christianizing.

Columbus landed on the Caribbean Island of Hispaniola, enslaving and carrying back to Europe many of the native population, forcibly converting them to Christianity.[1]

1. Jones, "Roots of Christian Nationalism."

***The Landing of Columbus*, by Albert Bobbett (1877). Public domain.**

Because English immigrants knew very little about agriculture in untamed, uncultivated soil and climate conditions, they relied on Native Americans to teach them how best to grow corn and vegetables.

In the mid-eighteenth century, the population of the thirteen colonies—now the states of New Hampshire, Massachusetts, Connecticut, Rhode Island, New York, New Jersey, Pennsylvania, Delaware, Maryland, Virginia, North Carolina, South Carolina, and Georgia—consisted of French, Spanish, Dutch, and even Russian immigrants, who co-mingled with the earlier English immigrants. Other religious groups such as Mennonites, Huguenots, and Moravians also sought religious freedom and relief from persecution in the new world. Not only freedom to worship but also over-population in Europe and economic opportunities in the new world drew these immigrants to the vast, unexplored, untamed continent.

European countries wanted to make as many colonies as they were able, so they recruited similar sponsors to send colonists for business opportunities to enrich their coffers. The new immigrants or colonists had to pay taxes to their home countries. When England began to increase those taxes, the resistance cry of "taxation without representation" arose. Former subjects then won their freedom to form their own brand of representative government without a king or an established religion subject to the crown. They became citizens of an experimental form of representative government, modeled after the Roman Republic's and England's legal system.

The fifty-five delegates to the Constitutional Convention of 1787 were men of faith: Anglicans, Congregationalists, Methodists, Lutherans, two Catholics, and one Deist. The federal Constitution makes no reference to God, but the Declaration of Independence, written by Thomas Jefferson, makes this reference to God in the Preamble: "We hold these truths to be self-evident, that all men are created equal, that they are endowed by their Creator with certain unalienable Rights, that among these are Life, Liberty and the pursuit of Happiness."[2]

In a letter to the Danbury, Connecticut, Baptist church, Jefferson wrote that the legislature should "make no law respecting an establishment of religion, or prohibiting the free exercise thereof, thus building a wall of separation between Church and State."[3]

These basic rights were codified in the Bill of Rights and in the first of the ten Amendments to the Constitution, the first being Freedom of Religion, Speech, and the Press:

> Congress shall make no law respecting establishment of religion or prohibiting the free exercise thereof, abridging the freedom of speech or of the press, or the right of the people peaceably to assemble and to petition the government for a redress of grievances.[4]

The United States Constitution sets forth a system of representative governance that establishes an executive branch, a legislative branch, and a judicial branch. Even though people vote their choice for president and vice president for the executive branch, American citizens must choose electors who then come together

2. Rosen and Rubenstein, "Declaration."
3. Jefferson, "Letter to the Danbury."
4. Constitution of the United States, Amendment I.

in an electoral college to determine which candidate wins the election. A candidate might win the popular vote that takes place every four years, but electors choose who will be the president and vice president. Today, each of the fifty states selects electors who represent that state's popular choice for president, but party politics along with wheeling and dealing really determines the outcome of any presidential election.

The rationale given by our founding fathers for the electoral college was (1) to protect against demagogues and (2) to protect the right of Congress in the deliberation process. Although James Madison had mixed thoughts about the electoral college, he considered both the advantages and disadvantages:

- Advantage: The candidates should be personally known in their electoral district.
- Advantage: In some cases, the electors might be intentionally left to exercise their own judgment.
- Advantage: The elector is allowed to vote for his constituents' second choice if he sees that the chances for their constituents' first choice is hopeless.
- Disadvantage: Open to horse trading, smoke-filled rooms, and dishonesty.[5]

When the Constitution was written by him as well as others, Madison represented a southern state that had many slaves—thus a greater population than most northern states—but they could not vote. Madison suggested the three-fifths compromise so that slave-owning states could compete with northern states.

In spite of native Indians providing help to the early settlers, both the English and the American patriots recruited them to fight for their cause in the American Revolution and eventually took over their established territories. In Virginia, English settlers bought slaves from Africa to help them grow and harvest tobacco and cotton. So both Native Americans and slaves from Africa were exploited and abused.

5. Dewey, "Madison's Views," 140–41.

Yet slave-holding states then tipped the balance in presidential choices until after the Civil War.[6] Because this rationale no longer is relevant, some suggest that election by popular vote for president replace the electoral college system.

Elected presidents are to be called "Mister" or "Madame" (if we ever elect a woman president), and their functions are:

- to honorably represent the people of the United States with foreign governments
- to head the military
- to approve or reject laws created by Congress
- to appoint judges to federal courts and the Supreme Court.

Two branches of Congress are to write laws; courts adjudicate the laws and create checks and balances so that the executive branch cannot run away with power.

In the almost three centuries since the signing of the Declaration of Independence and the signing of the Constitution, democracy, the American experiment, has worked, sometimes as it was intended, sometimes contrary to what was intended.

What has been the American dream? Our founding fathers described the American dream in the Bill of Rights as a "pursuit of happiness." They believed that a productive society could only flourish if we offered equal rights, including the worship of "God as I understand him."[7] The first pilgrims wanted freedom to worship. Today, others dream of finding productive and meaningful work; some want their children to have better education; still others want to be respected because of different skin color or a different belief system. American citizens expect not to be persecuted and to live without fear.

But these rights have not always been equal. At first, the rights were only for white Americans from European descent.[8]

6. Kelkar, "Electoral College is Vestige."

7. Step three of The Twelve Steps, as quoted in Webb, *Tree of Renewed Life*, 12.

8. Jones, "Roots of Christian Nationalism."

Native Americans, African Americans, women, and Asians have had to fight for those rights. Today their hopes are being dashed as they fear daily that ICE agents might handcuff them and imprison them in unsanitary detention centers. Native Americans have been discriminated against and sent to live in reservations in the West. African Americans were slaves and second-class citizens until Congress passed the Thirteenth, Fourteenth, and Fifteenth Amendments to the Constitution. Under the current administration racism once again threatens those freedoms.

The United States of America has survived the War of 1812, the Spanish–American War, the Civil War, the first and second World Wars, the Great Depression, 9/11, and the influx of immigrants, including Irish immigrants during the potato famine, Jews fleeing Germany and Russia, and immigrants from Eastern Europe, China, Mexico, and many others seeking refuge from authoritarian regimes and a chance at the American dream. The Statue of Liberty welcomes each new prospective citizen with their aspirations to share in the American experimental dream.

We, the American people, somehow have lost some of our high ideals of equal justice and fairness for all. John Mason, a Puritan captain, said after they massacred the Pequot tribe, "God laughed his Enemies and the Enemies of his People to Scorn, making them as a fiery oven . . . thus did the Lord judge among the Heathen, filling the Place with dead bodies."[9]

Yes, we can now worship in any way or no way. We want an education, a good job, and to earn enough money to purchase a decent house, buy an automobile, and maybe have guaranteed healthcare. Along with aiming to achieve more of this revised American dream for oneself and one's family, Americans seem more concerned about the loss of the common good and doing what is best for me. In the process, happiness has become elusive and drug abuse has risen, along with hate crimes, gun violence, and suicides, as well as declines in church attendance. Morality, honesty, integrity, and decency are no longer sought-after American values.

9. Claiborne and Haw, *Jesus for President*, 173.

Senator Robert F. Kennedy expressed it this way: "Too much and for too long, we seem to have surrendered personal excellence and community values in the mere accumulation of material things."[10]

One can say that the light began to dim during the greatest generation, the generation that gave us congressmen like John McCain, who acted in the nation's best interests, not his own, or George Herbert Walker Bush, who believed and instilled in his family that loving the Lord your God with all your heart, mind, and strength, and your neighbor as yourself, is the greatest commandment. Under his presidency, he dedicated the last of the stained-glass windows in the National Cathedral. Since the day was dark and dreary, looking up he couldn't see the beautiful Rose Window above him. Only with the sun shining through it could one gaze at its magnificence. On the day of his funeral service, his pastor, the Rev. Russell Levenson, said, "We see it backlit by the sun. It dazzles in astonishing splendor and reminds us that without faith we too are but stained glass windows in the dark."[11]

David Frum describes a set of weaknesses visible today: the discontent of those feeling left out, the rise in violence, irresponsibility of elites, insulation of the wealthy, and arrogance of party leaders.[12] The majority of them are white middle class churchgoing folks living in rural America, most without college degrees. As the culture around them changes they feel discounted, battered, and angry.

Janet Ruth believes that Christianity has been watered down in America. She writes in her book *One Nation Under God*,

> As the diversity of religious beliefs in the United States has grown, the common ground of religious identity has been stretched almost to the point of being nonexistent. What we have left is a nameless, faceless, generic God—a God of many definitions and choices—a God whose only

10. Quoted in Brown, "Man Does Not Live," para. 17.
11. PBS News, "Rev. Russell Levenson," 6:50.
12. Frum, *Trumpocracy*, 12–13.

> power is to solemnize occasions, inspire commitment, and set us apart from godless nations.[13]

Janet Ruth expressed what many Christians have deplored from the time of our founding fathers. Throughout our nation's history, these Christians have held that the United States of America was founded on Christian values and ideals and, therefore, we should be Christian nation. To be a true American one must be a Jesus follower.

13. Ruth, *One Nation Under God*, 45.

15

Divisions in American Christianity

THE TREND AWAY FROM established denominations began in the mid-nineteenth century with the rise of fundamentalism and Pentecostalism. Fundamentalism began as a reaction to Charles Darwin's *Origin of Species*, which was published in England in 1859. Darwin introduced a scientific theory that mankind evolved over a long period of time through evolution, changing the timeline of when humans appeared on the earth, contrary to the account in the book of Genesis in the Bible.

Early in the twentieth century theologians studying the Bible challenged the inerrancy of the Genesis passages in a movement called modernism. The reaction to modernism in American Christian churches was led by Dwight Moody, the Bible Institute, and Dallas Theological Seminary. The reaction—in the form of insistence on biblical inerrancy—was strongest in the southern states of Tennessee, Kentucky, Mississippi, and Alabama. Some of these states passed laws that evolution could not be taught in public schools. In Tennessee the law was called the Butler Act.[1]

When Princeton Theological Seminary published *The Fundamentals: A Testimony to the Truth*, fundamentalism was born, eventually becoming evangelicalism. This event created an age

1. Discussed in Melton et al., "Christian Fundamentalism."

of upheaval in society. In Protestant churches the result was the beginning of the Social Gospel movement, addressing issues of social justice by rethinking what Jesus said and taught. Its leaders shared many concerns with progressive reformers of the day: hunger, poverty, slums, poor quality schools, and the exploitation of workers. Walter Rauschenbusch, a Baptist pastor, was among the most active and was admired by my grandfather Bishop Charles Williams. Rauschenbusch urged people to help build the kingdom of God on earth, to follow Jesus' moral teachings, and to overcome selfish indifference. His writings influenced many later civil rights advocates, including Martin Luther King Jr., who named Rauschenbusch as one of his role models.[2]

As American Christian churches were being challenged to care for the least of these in society, there were political and judicial repercussions that culminated in the Scopes trial, or Monkey Trial, of 1925.

In order to challenge the Tennessee law, the concerned churches asked the American Civil Liberties Union (ACLU) to convince substitute teacher John Scopes to claim that he taught evolution because he was using a textbook to teach biology that had a chapter on evolution. William Jennings Bryan, seeking publicity for himself, defended the state law, whereas Clarence Darrow defended Scopes, who was eventually fined one hundred dollars when he lost the case. A movie entitled *Inherit the Wind* fanned the flames.

My interest in the Scopes trial occurred in my senior year in high school—when American Christians were obsessed with the trial—along with my growing interest in chemistry and astronomy. My thesis to this day is that science and evolution are compatible. Yet, even now, in the twenty-first century, the division still exists.

The fundamentalist theological movement has led to the formation of the Plymouth Brethren, Jerry Falwell, the Moral Majority, the Tea Party, Bob Jones and Liberty Universities, and teaching creationism or intelligent design alongside evolution in

2. According to a plaque about Martin Luther King Jr. on the wall of the Museum of the Bible.

some southern schools. Banning some books in schools and libraries, anti-vaccination, and renewed interest in the Scopes trial in 2025—the hundred-year anniversary of that notorious trial—all indicate that the battle between science and fundamentalism is very much alive. Four hundred or more attacks on science have occurred during the first six months of the current administration.[3]

Pentecostalism began with the Holiness movement in the nineteenth century, alongside fundamentalism, and grew exponentially in the twentieth and twenty-first centuries. Denominations such as the Assemblies of God, Christian Missionary Alliance, and Gospel churches are all considered Pentecostal.

During the latter half of the twentieth century, a phenomenon called the Toronto Blessing, led by Randy Clark, swept from Canada to the United States, bringing frequent occurrences of being slain in the Holy Spirit and transforming lives for Christ. This blessing—called charismatic after the word *charisma*, meaning a Holy Spirit gift of power to individuals for the good of the church—touched many worshiping individuals who profess being reborn, can speak in tongues, can prophesy, and believe in faith healing and miracles. Charismatic churches are now the fastest growing churches in the twenty-first century.

Charismatic renewal of churches impacted Roman Catholics as well. Beginning at Duquesne University in Pittsburgh in the 1960s and spreading to Episcopal and Presbyterian churches around the country, the movement led to many being deeply touched and transformed by the Holy Spirit during the seventies and eighties, myself included. Although never slain in the Spirit—as many were during that period—I was profoundly impacted and was led to membership in the Order of St. Luke, a healing ministry, and to attending Francis MacNutt's prayer ministry in Florida. When laying hands on people for healing, I have experienced the spiritual phenomenon of speaking in tongues. Two of my books, one on the history of the healing ministry, and one describing the process, resulted. My healing journey has called me into leading mission training teams internationally in substance misuse and

3. Wilkins, "Report Details," para. 1.

recovery and becoming a prayer healer as well as acquiring expertise in helping individuals and families heal from codependence.

In the late twentieth century, alongside the rise of the Pentecostal and charismatic movements, the biblical prophetic movement introduced dispensationalism, an extreme form of premillennialism that includes a concept of the rapture. In 1970, Hal Lindsey, a graduate of Dallas Theological Seminary, wrote the book *The Late Great Planet Earth.* This book was followed by Tim Lahaye's *Left Behind* series of books. Their books were based on interpretations and assumptions made from their study of the prophetic books of the Bible.[4]

Today, eschatology theories are prevalent among U.S. Protestants in evangelical and historically Black traditions. Respondents reported their beliefs in a Pew survey conducted on April 11–17, 2022, according to the following chart, when they responded to the question, "Do you believe we are living in the end times?"

4. Jeremiah, *Great Disappearance*, x.

U.S. Protestants in Evangelical and Historically Black Traditions Especially Likely to Believe Humanity Is "Living in the End Times."
Do you believe we are living in the end times?

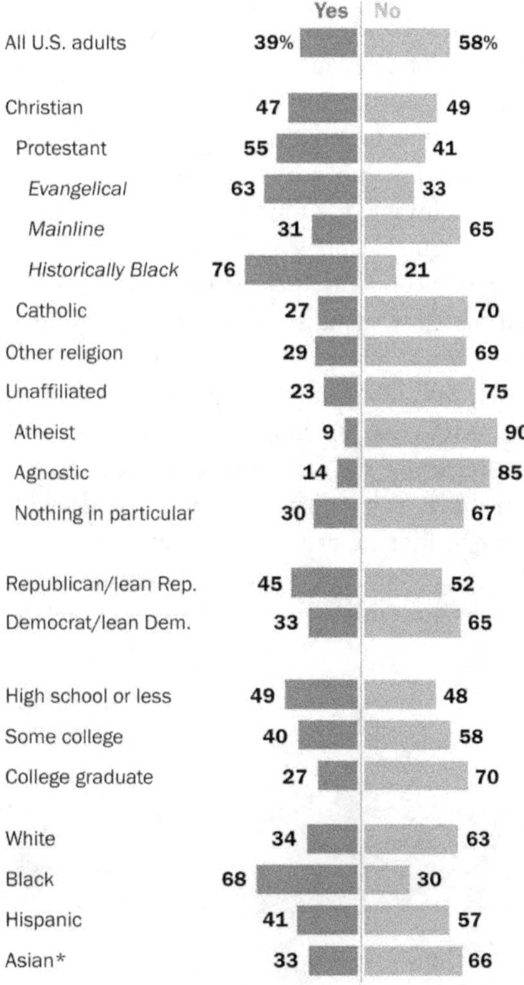

***Estimates for Asian adults are representative of English speakers only. Note: Those who did not answer are not shown. White, Black and Asian adults include those who report being only one race and are not Hispanic. Hispanics are of any race. "Other religion" includes those who identify as Jewish, Muslim, Buddhist, Hindu, or with another world religion or other non-Christian faith. Pew Research Center. Washington, DC. December 7, 2022.**

Fortunately, God has spared me from extreme and fringe theologies that have enticed believers like me through similar renewal experiences. However, I can understand why, without apostolic grounding and spiritual guidance, one could succumb to false and dangerous heretical beliefs. Also, during the Enlightenment period of church history, any man could read and interpret biblical passages. When I was a seminary student, we were often assigned a passage of the Bible, to research how that passage has been interpreted through church history, while studying the intent of the author and the culture at the time the passage was written. Also, we studied the original Hebrew or Greek meaning of the words.

This intense theological study, which most pastors learn to do in a certified seminary, along with the Holy Spirit's interventions, have grounded me in historical orthodox theology as well as living responsively to God's calling to do justice, love mercy, and walk humbly with Jesus. Now I'm ringing the alarm, calling American Christians to recognize the critical need to move away from any fringe apostasy that claims that America was founded as and/or should become their brand of a Christian nation. One such aberration—the New Apostolic Reformation, an extreme form of Christian nationalism—now threatens both Christianity and the nation.

16

Christian Nationalism and Zionism in America

AT FIRST, THE ANABAPTIST churches, the Mennonites, the Church of the Brethren, and the Amish led the way in steering away from an involvement with politics and culture. The most extreme were the Amish—and still are. The other established denominations in America held to creedal Christianity. These include but are not limited to, the Roman Catholic Church, the Protestant Episcopal Church, the Anglican Church of North America, the Southern Baptist Church, African-American churches, the United Methodist Church, the Evangelical Lutheran Church, the Presbyterian Church of the USA, the United Church of Christ, the Moravian Church, and the Seventh Day Adventist Church, among others.

Throughout America's experimental history there have been attempts by Christian groups to make America Christian, including through educational materials. Christian nationalism in its various forms has been defined as a political and cultural ideology.[1] Andrew Whitehead and Sam Perry, in their book *Taking America Back for God*, describe American Christian nationalism as American idolatry of power that has nothing to do with loving

1. Some organizations and movements that resist Christian nationalism as a political and cultural ideology include Red Letter Christians, Reclaiming Jesus, Vote Common Good, and Christians Against Christian Nationalism.

your neighbor and that views non–natural born citizens as "unworthy" of citizenship.[2] Christians against Christian Nationalism provides the following definition:

> Christian nationalism is a cultural framework that idealizes and advocates a fusion of Christianity with American civic life. Christian nationalism contends that America has been and should always be distinctively "Christian" from top to bottom—in its self-identity, interpretations of its own history, sacred symbols, cherished values, and public policies—and it aims to keep it that way.[3]

I prefer the meaning that has been discussed herein: the synchronization of church and state, when a prevailing religion, Christianity, entwines with the federal government, thus denying other ways of worshiping as null and void.

Remember that in Jerusalem at the time when Jesus began to preach and teach, the Pharisees were both spiritual and political leaders, many in league with the Roman prelates sent by Caesar to keep the peace. Although Jesus often dialogued with and challenged the Pharisees, he did so to remind them that they had veered from God's domain ways.

Christian Zionism began in the nineteenth century to find a way for scattered Jews to find a home in the land of Palestine, then controlled by the Ottoman Empire. After WWI the empire dissolved and Britain then took control of the land. The British government sought to establish Israel's independence through the Balfour Declaration. Under the leadership of the League of Nations, the Jewish people who had illegally immigrated to the land of Palestine needed a home. Before WWII thousands of Jews left Germany when Hitler took over. After WWII, evangelical Christians in Great Britain determined that displaced Jews should reclaim the land in Palestine. The publication and promotion of the Scofield Reference Bible, whose interpretation of Gen 12:3—"I will bless them that bless thee and curse him that

2. Whitehead, "3 Threats," para. 3.

3. Christians Against Christian Nationalism, "What Is Christian Nationalism?"

curseth thee" (KJV)—became the calling cry for the creation of Israel. Jews, these evangelical Christians believed, were chosen by God to live in the land of Palestine. Once that land is returned fully to Jews, the closer will be Jesus' return (dispensationalism). In 1948, the Jewish people came from all over to claim their promised land.[4] One of them, a cousin of mine, raised a Quaker, heard the call. She married a Jewish man from New York City. They went to Israel on their honeymoon to live in a kibbutz and restore the land, then occupied by Palestinians—many of whom were and are still Christians.

Then, as now, Israelis and Palestinians have fought throughout history for their right to live in the land that Abraham was sent by God to claim. Remember Abraham had at least two sons: his firstborn, Ishmael, born by his concubine, Hagar, and Isaac, born to Sarah in her old age. God promised Abraham that he would be the father of many nations (Gen 17). Both sons populated the land Abraham claimed for God.

But for many evangelical Christians, especially those caught up in Christian nationalism, being a Christian means unquestionable support for the nation of Israel. Yet, the current Israeli administration wants to get rid of all the Palestinian people living on what they consider to be land promised by God for them, even though under the British agreement the Jewish people in 1948 were only promised 56 percent of the land. Their intention has been to humiliate Arab Muslims and Arab Christians, grab their land, treat them as inferior, send them to another country, or kill them. Any time humans made in the image of God are so treated our Lord cries out, *Stop*. But, if the current peace treaty holds, there may be a chance for a two-state solution.

Today, from the New Apostolic Reformation, or Dominionism, to the Reawaken America events, these Christian nationalist and Zionist organizations attract large audiences in many American towns and villages, connecting with those caught up in a cult of a media-savvy charismatic personalities that includes pastors

4. See Timeless Myths, "What Was Israel," and Encyclopaedia Britannica, "Israeli-Palestinian Conflict Explained."

as well as conservative Republicans and many conservative Christians. These devotees believe we should restore prayer and Bible studies in our schools or, at the very least, display "In God we trust" posters in each classroom and courtroom. Adherents were present at the January 6, 2021 insurrection holding the Bible, the American flag, and/or the Appeal to Heaven flag, the flag of the New Apostolic Reformation. Considering themselves citizen patriots, they wrongly believed that they were being faithful Christians by storming the Capitol building, pepper-spraying and killing policemen to take over the government.

Their eschatological beliefs range from premillennialism to postmillennialism.[5] But they are attempting to make America a Christian nation to be ready for Jesus' return. Settling the Jewish people in the holy land of Palestine and now Israel is also one of the tasks to be accomplished, and that means dealing with the native Palestinians, who are treated like the Native Americans were treated when white Europeans arrived to take over the land where they had lived for centuries.

Remember when our land was settled by the pilgrims, then becoming the United States of America? Starting with Thomas Jefferson—a deist by faith—our founding fathers did not want the new American nation to be a Christian nation. Most American citizens today may wish sometimes that our democratic government were not so messy but cherish their freedoms to worship or not worship. However, those caught up in the vestiges of the New Apostolic Reformation, Christian nationalism, and Zionism threaten both American Christianity and our democracy.

5. Boedy, *Seven Mountains Mandate*, 47.

17

Danger: The New Apostolic Reformation

The New Apostolic Reformation,[1] or NAR, was named by C. Peter Wagner, a former professor at Fuller Theological Seminary. Dr. Wagner believed in a form of dominion theology, the theology that began to surface in charismatic Pentecostal churches in the 1980s. Wagner bought into the theory that governments are ruled by demonic spirits and that Christians need to fight a spiritual warfare to take dominion over all the institutions of countries. In further examination, this extreme version of Christian nationalism has the earmarks of several heresies: *Manichaeism*, because of their belief that we're in a spiritual warfare against the evils of the culture; *Gnosticism*, because they believe they have special knowledge given to them by God; and *Montanism*, because they possess spiritual gifts through prophecy. Their dominion theology is a form of Reconstructionism that derived originally from the teachings of R. J. Rushdoony in the 1960s and 1970s.[2] It focuses on man instituting the rule of the law of God for governments and institutions, with their perceived biblical mandate. Along with this mandate, they believe that we are in the second apostolic age, where God calls apostles and prophets to leadership in churches. There is even

1. Described in the introduction of Boedy, *Seven Mountain Mandate.*
2. Wikipedia, "Dominion Theology."

an International Coalition of Apostolic Leadership website where apostolic leaders may register. Voices of the Apostles conferences are planned in many areas—one planned in my own town. Randy Clark, of the Toronto Blessing, will be one of the lead speakers.

Wagner convinced enough charismatic, Pentecostal, and evangelical nondenominational congregations about the validity of this new apostolic period of church history that the NAR has become the fastest growing heretical Christian nationalist movement, with its Gnostic flavor and millennial eschatology. Its chosen leaders receive secret instructions directly from God. Converted congregations set up twenty-four-hour prayer vigils as God's warriors in a spiritual battle to defeat the demons that have taken over societal institutions. Congregants and leaders seek political participation, including running for office and serving in local, state, and national government as well as serving in the judiciary. They believe that God is calling them to stand on top of and then dismantle and take over the seven institutions—sometimes referred to as "spheres"[3]—of American society: government, education, business, the media, family, arts and entertainment, and religion. This became the Seven Mountain Mandate, which was introduced to Charlie Kirk by Rob McCoy, a megachurch pastor, and encouraged by Lance Wallnau, the father of Dominionism.[4] Wallnau added an eighth sphere, "the mountain of me"—in other words, "self-mastery."[5] Kirk then became the proponent of the Seven Mountain Mandate to the Trump administration and Trump family.

Early in the first Trump presidency, many of the NAR prophets and apostles approached the White House and asked to come and pray over the newly elected president. Among the prophet and apostle leaders was Paula White-Cain, who has since been chosen to be the senior advisor to the White House Faith Office in the second Trump term. They also gathered to pray with him for two hours before the January 6 insurrection. Those who prayed also convinced the new president that he was chosen by God to restore

3. Boedy, *Seven Mountain Mandate*, 13.

4. Boedy, *Seven Mountain Mandate*, 17.

5. Boedy, *Seven Mountain Mandate*, 17.

America as a great Christian nation. So convinced was he that he decided to become one of them and chose his new cabinet partly due to their commitment to make America the Christian nation they envisioned.

When Donald Trump was arrested and indicted by a grand jury, his followers waved their Appeal to Heaven flags and compared the trial to Jesus' trial and crucifixion. When a sniper's bullet only grazed his ear, his followers believed along with him that God spared him to make America great again according to NAR and Project 2025 criteria.

After Charlie Kirk, who founded Turning Point USA, was killed, a special remembrance day drew ninety thousand citizens, and seventy thousand filled the State Farm Stadium in Glendale, Arizona, with President Trump and members of his administration giving speeches. Erika, his grieving widow, made a powerful moving testimony to the couple's Christian faith and marriage, but she made no mention of their concern for immigrants, the poor, and the lost. Even though President Trump in his speech said that Charlie Kirk had tried to convince him to love his enemies, the president admitted that he hated his enemies. President Trump, with full endorsement of the Supreme Court and political colleagues, has weaponized the Justice Department to prosecute anyone who is not loyal, criticizes him, or has prosecuted him. Before his unfortunate assassination, Charlie Kirk had convinced enough young men to elect Trump by strong-arming them—in what he referred to as a debate—into voting for him. Now we see his bronze statue everywhere. A special day has been created to remember him, while Americans' freedom of speech and religion are corrupted.

Just how many of those who espouse the theology of the NAR apostasy work in the White House have the ear of the president, who is reputed to make decisions based on the last person he listens to? His deputy chief of staff, Stephen Miller, has an "affinity for white nationalism"[6] and was the lead author of the 2025 plan put together by the Heritage Foundation, one of the streams of

6. SPLC, "Leaked Emails," article title.

Christian nationalism. J. D. Vance joined a Catholic church affiliated with Catholic integralism. According to Matthew Cressler, who is a Catholic historian, professor, and director of the Crossroads Project at Princeton University, their theology is racist and sexist and does away with any separation of church and state.[7] Pete Hegseth has on his arms the tattoo of "Deus Vult," or "God wills it," considered a Crusader battle cry. He also distributes a coin with the Crusader cross.[8] Now many believe—as does President Trump—that using America's military and National Guard to coerce, arrest, and even murder without due process is the Christian way. That's not the Jesus way.

The next time you are in Washington, DC, visit the Capitol buildings where representatives and senators have their offices, and note those who have the Appeal to Heaven flags outside their doors, especially the chairman of the House of Representatives. Ginni Thomas, the wife of Supreme Court Justice Clarence Thomas, served on the Turning Point board of directors.[9] She also flies the Appeal to Heaven flag.

Rest uneasily that these men and women are under the cult-like spell of the New Apostolic Reformation. If they were to gather to march down the streets of the capital carrying those flags—much like the Ku Klux Klan members did—and the color of your skin is dark or you are an immigrant, you would have every right to be afraid.

In 2023, 30 percent of two thousand Americans surveyed were favorable to the Seven Mountain Mandate and thought that Christian values should be "solely and explicitly endorsed by the government." But a year later, that percentage had increased to 41 percent.[10]

Also, in a 2024 Public Religion Institute survey, 29 percent of those interviewed were strongly aligned with the ideology of Christian nationalism.

7. Boedy, *Seven Mountain Mandate*, Introduction.

8. Ryan, "Holy Warrior," para. 20.

9. Boedy, *Seven Mountain Mandate*, 18.

10. Boedy, *Seven Mountain Mandate*, 3.

- Two-thirds of that group agreed that "God ordained Donald Trump to be the winner of the 2024 election."
- More than one-third of that group believed that Americans "may need to resort to violence in order to save our country."
- Nearly two-thirds of that group agreed that "immigrants are invading our country and replacing our cultural and ethnic background."[11]

If the past three-year growth of the NAR movement and the ninety thousand who attended Charlie Kirk's remembrance event and NAR's most recent convention are indicators, then if those same pollsters were to do another survey they might find an alarming number of Americans are following a false Christ. Jesus warned his followers to watch out for those who claim to be his followers but are not. If that same survey could also include a modified Likert scale based on Jesus' teachings, assessing how these individuals really follow what Jesus taught and what his apostles and prophets preach, alarm bells would ring out everywhere. Instead, NAR adherents are too busy gutting institutions in the process of taking them over.

Some call Christian nationalism—especially the NAR version—a fascist movement; some, a white supremacy movement. Either way, in their spiritual warfare that espouses violence to achieve their goal, the NAR will co-opt both American Christianity and American democracy. Many Christian nationalist devotees are also caught up in Christian Zionism, supporting genocide of the Palestinian people, claiming that the land where both the Jewish people of Israel and the Palestinian people—both Christians and Muslims live—belongs to Israel. God loves both the people of Israel, now a nation-state, and the Palestinian people.

To return to real citizenship in God's domain involves going back to stories Jesus taught in the Bible and examining the lives of those who exemplify what true citizenship looks like, according to God's plan.

11. Byrd, "New Poll."

PART VI

Citizenship Revisited

18

Citizenship Examples

So then you are no longer strangers and sojourners, but you are fellow citizens with the saints and members of the household of God, built upon the foundation of the apostles and prophets, Christ Jesus himself being the cornerstone.

—EPHESIANS 2:19–20 (NRSV)

CITIZENS IN GOD'S DOMAIN are like points of light that stand out in the world, living their lives as followers of Jesus.

Imagine the layout of a map of historical periods with points of light where these citizens might shine out. Besides the twelve apostles and Paul, some of these names might appear: Augustine, Benedict, Dorothy Day, Theodosius, Anselm, Anthony, Bernard of Clairvaux, Origen, Henri Nouwen, Athanasius, Teresa of Avila, Karl Barth, Benjamin Nzimbi, Menno Simons, Francis MacNutt, Joan Chittister, Thomas Merton, Martin Luther King Jr., and Jim Wallis. You name others.

Let's examine the map in depth to find out more about some special points of light who exemplify what Christian citizenship is all about.

***Points of Light*, created by the author with Microsoft Copilot**

AN ITALIAN FRIAR: FRANCIS OF ASSISI

Francesco was born in Umbria in AD 1181 into the family of a wealthy cloth merchant named Pietro di Bernardone.[1] Pietro's wife had their infant son baptized Giovanni (named after John the Baptist). But his father renamed him Francesco because he loved everything French. Francesco grew up with a loving and happy disposition, but was never a good student. Instead, he joined a group and aspired, like them, to become a knight. He then fought in the war of Assisi against Perugia and was taken prisoner, surviving for a year in a dungeon before he was ransomed. Afterward, he prepared to fight in the Fourth Crusade and even ordered a tailor to make him a magnificent cloak, requesting a suit of armor

1. Several sources informed my discussion of St. Francis, including Akin, "Who Was St. Francis"; Encyclopaedia Britannica, "St. Francis of Assisi"; and Wikipedia, "Francis of Assisi."

decorated with gold. However, God called him to repent, so Francesco never wore his new clothes. When he saw an old church in disrepair, he believed Christ was telling him to repair the church. Hearing those words, he misinterpreted them to mean the building itself. He sold some of his father's cloth goods to get cash to repair the church building. When his angry father found out, he dragged Francesco to the bishop, who told him to return the money. When Francesco paid back the money to the bishop, he removed all his clothes and gave them also to the bishop. From then on, he wore rags and became a wandering preacher.

Those who followed Francesco gave up their worldly possessions, donned brown hooded robes, and became beggars to follow Jesus. They became known as friars. Each morning, Francesco would send them off saying something like this, "Go preach the gospel and use words if you have to." One day, a thief stole one of their brown hoods. A brother ran after him and gave him his robe as well.

Francesco became known for his peacemaking between warring districts. Although he didn't actually write it, this peace prayer has been attributed to him:

> Lord, make me an instrument of your peace.
> Where there is hatred, let me bring love.
> Where there is offence, let me bring pardon.
> Where there is discord, let me bring union.
> Where there is error, let me bring truth.
> Where there is doubt, let me bring faith.
> Where there is despair, let me bring hope.
> Where there is darkness, let me bring your light.
> Where there is sadness, let me bring joy.
> O Lord, grant that I may not so much seek
> to be consoled as to console,
> to be understood as to understand,
> to be loved as to love,
> for it is in giving that one receives,
> it is in self-forgetting that one finds,
> it is in forgiving that one is forgiven,
> it is in dying that one awakens to eternal life.[2]

2. Wikipedia, "Prayer of St. Francis."

Francesco and his brothers followed Jesus by going out two by two in their rags to share the good news of Jesus Christ, living out Francis's dream of resurrecting a church body that had fallen into disrepair and disgrace. Often, they were called madmen. Missiles of rocks and mud were thrown at them. They suffered much pain and persecution. Francis himself endured so much suffering that the marks of Christ's wounds appeared on his own body and he became blind.

The Franciscan monastic order that he began is still alive and well today, the brothers showing us all by their vows of poverty and service what it means to be citizens of God's domain.

AN INDIAN FROM YUGOSLAVIA: MOTHER TERESA

On August 26, 1910, in Skopje, Yugoslavia, Agnes Gonxha Bojaxhiu was born.[3] When she was eighteen, she entered the Loretto Sisters Convent in Dublin, Ireland so she could do mission work in Bengal, India. There she adopted the name Teresa, after Thérèse of Lisieux, whose spiritual journey, recorded in *The Story of a Soul*, she may have studied. On a train to Darjeeling in 1946, she heard a call from God to serve him among the poorest of the poor in the Calcutta slums. Others soon joined her, and the order of the Missionaries of Charity was born. Soon after, she made a link with the National Council of Catholic Women. In 1979, she received the Nobel Peace Prize, and from then until now the Missionaries of Charity has grown so that there are five hundred houses located in ninety-seven countries.

Much has been written about Mother Teresa as she embodies the Beatitudes in her life's work. Always finding an opportunity to raise money for her homes for the poor (several built near garbage dumps) she connected the rich and comfortable with the poorest of the poor, especially the poor who lay dying.

3. Several sources informed my discussion of Mother Teresa, including Egan and Egan, *Blessed Are You*; Encyclopaedia Britannica, "Mother Teresa"; Wikipedia, "Mother Teresa"; Biography.com, "Mother Teresa Biography."

She wrote the following litany about who Jesus was for her:

Jesus is the Word made Flesh
Jesus is the Bread of Life
Jesus is the Victim offered for our sins on the Cross
Jesus is the Sacrifice offered at the Holy Mass for the sins of the world and mine
Jesus is the Word—to be spoken
Jesus is the Truth—to be told
Jesus is the Way—to be walked
Jesus is the Light—to be lit
Jesus is the Life—to be lived
Jesus is the Love—to be loved
Jesus is the Joy—to be shared
Jesus is the Sacrifice—to be offered
Jesus is the Peace—to be given
Jesus is the Bread of Life—to be eaten
Jesus is the Hungry—to be fed
Jesus is the Thirsty—to be satiated
Jesus is the Naked—to be clothed
Jesus is the Homeless—to be taken in
Jesus is the Sick—to be healed
Jesus is the Lonely—to be loved[4]

When Mother Teresa died, everyone around the world seemed mesmerized watching Princess Diana's funeral from every television. Mother Teresa's death received no fanfare or media attention. Their lifestyles were on a different plane. Princess Diana lived a life of fame and luxury as a member of the British royal family. To her credit, after meeting Mother Teresa, she took on many charitable causes that were unpopular, such as visiting those with AIDS. But she never lived among them, as Mother Teresa did. However, angels must have sounded the fanfare when they received the diminutive nun in a white sari into heaven, as Jesus welcomed her into the fullness of his time for setting an example of servanthood in her life on earth.

Most of us may never become as well-known as these two citizens, and certainly will not have saint days or holidays named

4. Egan and Egan, *Blessed Are You*, 43–44.

for us. Many of us belong to denominations or churches that are opposed to singling out one person's ministry over another. Mennonites, especially, don't believe in singling out individuals for sainthood status.

But citizens of the domain of God have made a difference throughout the ages of God's domain and provided course correction when their fellow humans have gotten off course.

Bonhoeffer's name lights up in the twentieth century; his way of following Jesus is an example for us Christians today.

A GERMAN THEOLOGIAN: DIETRICH BONHOEFFER

On February 4, 1906, in Berlin, Germany, Dietrich was born into an aristocratic family, one of eight children. His mother was a preacher at the court of Kaiser Wilhelm II and his father was a professor of psychiatry in Berlin. His family thought that Dietrich was headed to a musical career because of his gift as a pianist, but when Dietrich was fourteen years old, he announced that he wanted to become a minister and theologian. He followed this career path, becoming not only a pastor but a theological scholar. He spent a semester at Union Theological Seminary in New York in 1927, where his teaching and preaching attracted large audiences. His colleagues at Union tried to persuade him to stay in America. Instead, he returned to Germany to become a lecturer at the University of Berlin.

As the majority of German Christians were proclaiming their first allegiance to Adolf Hitler, Professor Bonhoeffer and his friends Karl Barth and Martin Niemöller, together with other pastors and theologians, took a prophetic stance and organized the Confessing Church. In 1934, Karl Barth wrote the Barmen Declaration, which declared allegiance first to Jesus Christ. Yet, many pastors who signed the Barmen Declaration also belonged to the Nazi party.

Pastor Bonhoeffer shines as a point of light above the others on our map because of his concern for the Jewish question. He stated that to be a disciple of Jesus Christ, we are called to act on behalf of others.[5] He acted to help German Jews escape from the gestapo. He also started an underground seminary to train pastors to serve the Confessing Church, focusing on the Christian community.[6] The gestapo shut down the seminary.

During this period, Professor Bonhoeffer wrote his book *Costly Discipleship*, stating,

> Cheap grace is the preaching of forgiveness without requiring repentance, baptism without church discipline, Communion without confession, absolution without confession. Cheap grace is grace without discipleship, grace without the cross, grace without Jesus Christ, living and incarnate.[7]

There are many gems of wisdom in this little book that has now become a Christian classic and required reading for seminary students. Here's another passage from this book that pertains to following Jesus:

> Follow me, run along behind me! That is all. To follow in his footsteps is something which is void of all content. It gives no intelligible programme for a way of life, no goal or ideal to strive after . . . No other significance is possible, since Jesus is the only significance. Besides Jesus nothing has any significance. He alone matters.[8]

As a pacifist, Pastor Bonhoeffer tried to oppose Nazism through persuasion but found that didn't work and joined a plot to overthrow and then assassinate Hitler. In April 1943, he was arrested and spent two years in prison where he wrote letters, poems, and many papers that his guards smuggled out of prison. Eventually, he was transferred to Buchenwald and then to Flossenbürg in 1945. One month before Germany surrendered, he was hanged.

5. Hale and Williams, "Is This a Bonhoeffer," para. 29.

6. Siegele-Wenschkewitz, "Christians Against Nazis," para. 9. See also, Granberg-Michaelson, "When Seminary."

7. Bonhoeffer, *Cost of Discipleship*, 47.

8. Bonhoeffer, *Cost of Discipleship*, 62–63.

Hermann Fischer-Hüllstrung, camp doctor at the Flossenbürg concentration camp who witnessed the hanging, described the scene as follows: "In almost fifty years that I have worked as a doctor, I have hardly ever seen a man die so entirely submissive to the will of God."[9]

The following is a quote attributed to Bonhoeffer that epitomizes living as a citizen of God's domain:

> God is not ashamed of the lowliness of human beings. God marches right in. He chooses people as his instruments and performs his wonders where one would least expect them. God is near to the lowliest; he loves the lost, the neglected, the unseemly, the excluded, the weak and the broken.[10]

Many Christian citizens are or were monastics, writers, and preachers who gave up worldly possessions for ministries with the poor, the dying, and the homeless; in contrast, Dietrich Bonhoeffer's witness stands out as someone who stood for Christ against the powerful Nazi regime. When he followed his call, he paid with his life. Another example could be Martin Luther King Jr., who led the movement for racial equality and was assassinated.

A RED-LETTER AMERICAN: SHANE CLAIBORNE

In addition to doing graduate work at Princeton Seminary, Shane Claiborne received an honorary degree in 2010 from his alma mater, Eastern University, prior to becoming a leading American peace and justice activist and leader. His Christian citizenship witness has included spending time in Calcutta with Mother Teresa and going to Iraq in 2003 to report on the devastation done by cluster bombs during the invasion. I heard his story firsthand during a visit to his Kensington home shortly after he returned. He has also led the effort to reduce gun violence by turning guns into garden tools. Most recently he visited Palestine and has become an

9. Bethge, *Dietrich Bonhoeffer*, 927.

10. Bonhoeffer, *Dietrich Bonhoeffer*, 342.

advocate for the people of Palestine. He wants the world to see Jesus with his people in the rubble, holding the broken and displaced women and children in his arms.

Shane started the Red Letter Christians Movement with the late Tony Campolo. I joined as a member to keep me grounded in my spiritual journey. Membership means commitment to live the lifestyle prescribed by Jesus in the Gospels and wearing a bracelet that says "Red Letter Christians" that leads to explaining to many people just what that means.

Shane also founded The Simple Way, an organization in the Kensington area of Philadelphia's inner city that has provided food and school supplies as well as a library for the children in their neighborhood. Shane and his wife and young son live in community in the same area. There you will find Shane in a brown cloak, like a Franciscan friar, when he isn't pounding guns into garden tools, writing, traveling, or speaking about peacemaking, social justice, and Jesus. He witnesses and prays with others at weapons factories and in the nation's capital and has been arrested on some of those occasions. Shane's books include *Jesus for President*, *Red Letter Revolution*, *Common Prayer*, *Follow Me to Freedom*, *Jesus, Bombs, and Ice Cream*, *Becoming the Answer to Our Prayers*, *Executing Grace*, *Beating Guns*, and *Rethinking Life*.

These Christian citizens as well as many others light the world for Christ in God's domain. But how do we follow in man's domain?

19

Man's Domain

"Behold, you are old and your sons do not walk in your ways; now appoint for us a king to govern us like all the nations." But the thing displeased Samuel when they said, "Give us a king to govern us." And Samuel prayed to the LORD. And the LORD said to Samuel, "Hearken to the voice of the people in all that they say to you; for they have not rejected you, but they have rejected me from being king over them."

—1 SAMUEL 8:5–7 (RSV)

WHEN MAN IN THE Old Testament book of Samuel asked for a king, God was not pleased, but he consented, warning them of the dangers. Human beings like to run things. Then, much too quickly, power and control take over. God's way is forgotten or sublimated.

Jesus understands this temptation, and it was one reason he taught humility and servanthood leadership. Some of Jesus' disciples—those who were of the Zealot party—expected the Messiah to fight their Roman occupiers. Instead, Jesus urged them to love their enemies and pray for those who persecuted them (Matt 5:43–48). He also said if someone slaps you on one cheek, turn the other cheek (Matt 5:39; Luke 6:29), and if someone steals your coat, give him your shirt. Challenging commandments even today.

Citizens of Palestine during Jesus' time on earth hated tax collectors and did not want to pay Roman taxes, but Jesus chose a tax collector, Matthew, to be one of his special disciples. When cornered by the Pharisees about paying taxes to Caesar, this is how Jesus responded: "Give back to Caesar what belongs to Caesar and give to God what belongs to God" (Matt 22:21 ERV).[1]

The Jewish people had their own coinage system and the Romans had theirs. The Pharisees, who didn't believe in paying Roman taxes, had entered into a temporary scheme with the Herodians (who were for paying the Roman taxes) that if they asked Jesus that question, they could trap him. If he sided with either of their views, he'd be arrested for treason immediately. But Jesus wasn't quite ready to be arrested. He recognized the trap and flattery and asked to see the denarius, a Roman coin with the emperor's face on it. He defused the trap and with this statement separated out life in man's domain with life in God's domain. Jesus often spoke to his disciples about the kind of kin-dom that he told them he was starting on earth, which was very different from the prevalent culture or government.

Richard Niebuhr describes how Christians can challenge the culture in which they live, accommodate to the culture, or practice their faith separate from the culture.[2] Niebuhr makes no ethical distinction between these positions but surmises a kind of dualism that can result. Throughout two thousand years of Christian history there have been extremes and variations of these positions of how a Christian functions with various governments and government leaders in a country and in the cultural times in which each Christian lives. This dualism can be good or bad, depending upon the human frailties of those involved. Today, we're in one of those extreme times when Christians need to speak out and act in nonviolent ways against the entwinement of church and state and heretical beliefs that are contrary to Jesus' way, truth, and life.

1. Taken from the Holy Bible: Easy-to-Read Version (ERV), International Edition © 2013, 2016 by Bible League International and used by permission.

2. Niebuhr, *Christ and Culture*.

20

Citizenship Choices for American Christians

Before reading this chapter to help you make decisions going forward, please go back and reread chapter 11: "Nazi Germany and One Church." Our friends in Germany today are warning Americans about the frightening parallels between what led up to what happened to Germany then and what is happening to America today. Witness the parallels of the actions of ICE agents to SS agents. Will this be the end of our grand experiment in democracy?

In the eighteenth century, historian Edward Gibbon claimed that when Christianity became a state religion under Constantine, the church and the state were distracted by religious factions that contributed to Rome's downfall.[1] If his hypothesis holds true, then our founding fathers were careful to put together a constitution that did not include sponsoring one religious belief over another. However, they still believed in God, calling him their great Creator.[2]

Americans have not learned from world history, from the perils of a country like Germany that succumbed to Hitler's charisma and false promises. But Germans today remember. Russell Moore, editor of *Christianity Today*, raised an alarm in his

1. Gibbon, *Decline and Fall*, 67.

2. Constitution of the United States, Preamble.

newsletter when Tucker Carlson hosted neo-Nazi Nick Fuentes on his podcast in 2025. Moore wrote,

> This matter is crucial for the future of the country, but the stakes are even higher for the church. It is well past time for the church of Jesus Christ to take this seriously. And the first step to seeing how to do so is to ask, "Why do so many evangelical pastors and leaders not take it seriously now?" The Bible will not sit alongside *Mein Kampf*. The cross will not yield to the swastika. We must ask right now: Jesus or Hitler? We cannot have both.[3]

We watch Putin's killing sprees with support of the Russian Orthodox patriarch with horror and our administration's appeasement with shame.

Americans have not learned from the days of McCarthyism in America, from the Scopes trial, from the treatment of Japanese Americans during WWII, from the treatment of Native Americans during the Jackson administration, from the years of the slavery of African Americans, or from all the children who have lost their lives because of being shot by other youth or deranged adults with the type of guns that soldiers in battle are trained to fire.

American Christians have not studied Christian history, and many who call themselves Christians do not follow either the compass of the Beatitudes or Jesus' commandment to love their neighbors, especially the sojourners or immigrants who are our neighbors.

American Christians had not experienced what it means to live under a dictator such as Stalin, Putin, or Orban until Trump was elected for a second term. They have not experienced what the people of Israel experienced when the Roman Empire conquered it or what the Palestinian people have experienced since Israel began to take over that land.

What action or inaction each American Christian decides to take in the future will depend on how we view our responsibilities as citizens under Christ's leadership.

The options are as follows:

3. Moore, "Church Better Start," para. 2.

1. We will only live in the domain of God while standing above and apart from our current cultural morass. We will not discuss the current political situation. All politicians are the same, so we won't vote. Instead, we'll just allow whatever will happen to happen and accept that it is God's will. We'll withdraw, become contemplatives, or join a monastic community.[4]
2. We'll continue to mix our political preferences and ideas with our Christian faith. We'll continue to support our current president no matter what he tweets or what executive decrees he proclaims. We will use him to get rid of abortion, close our borders, support ICE raids, grab children and ship all of them to a developing country or just make them disappear, impose tariffs on other countries, build up our military-industrial complex, make sure the wealthiest citizens don't have to pay taxes, and insist that the working class, the poor, and the sick make it on their own.
3. We will put our Christian values and beliefs to the test, becoming catalysts to educate, agitate, transform, refresh, rebuild, and recover our democracy. That may involve protesting, resisting, boycotting, or divesting, as well as political activism, while nurturing our own souls in community. We can be of the world but not in the world, be willing to be called radical, socialist, or communist and endure the slings and arrows of a culture that has gone awry. Lastly, we need to be ready to suffer and be persecuted because we follow Jesus.

Reclaiming the importance of absolute truth, creedal truth as well as biblical truth, will be essential for how our citizenship as followers of Jesus will or will not help us survive and thrive. Along with reclaiming truth, taking seriously the words of the Apostles' or Nicene Creeds and the Lord's Prayer will lead to reinstating our Christian values that have sustained our democracy.

If we throw away the idea of truth, life is no longer safe. When truth is no longer valued, we cannot expect any society to respect

4. Dreher, *Benedict Option*.

absolute truth and thus negate those who are hurt when their truth is violated.

If we throw away the idea that anything is absolutely true or each of us relies on our own version of the truth or lying becomes accepted, our great American democracy will crumble just as the Roman Empire did. Well-meaning Christians will be complacent in that happening. We can either adopt the first option above; give in, give up, and say that we are living in the eschaton and God is in control, allowing the corruption, lies, and manipulation to continue unchallenged; or adopt the third option: fight for justice, honesty, and integrity in our politicians, calling for them to be more compassionate, merciful, just, honest, and fair. In Matt 23, Jesus publicly condemned the Pharisees and the scribes (the lawyers), and he did not mince words or try to be nice. We need to do the same to Trump and other politicians. Opposition and persecution may result when we stand up and speak out against their hypocrisy. Red Letter Christians, Reclaiming Jesus, Vote the Common Good, and Christians Against Christian Nationalism have begun this process.

But we first need to get the speck out of our own eyes, the absoluteness of our political biases and our sacrilegious theologies. On the one hand, some Christians have been co-opted into a cult of personality and have neglected to be transformed by Jesus and what he taught and how he wants us to live; on the other hand, party politics, LGBTQ+ rights, as well as pro-life rights also dangerously distract us from our biblical and creedal faith, weakening our allegiance to God.

Just because the United States idolizes a capitalist way of commerce doesn't mean that capitalism is acceptable in the dwelling of God. In fact, if we follow Jesus' teachings, his way turns out to be more radical than socialism. Early Christian communities held everything in common and lived out the Beatitudes in doing so. Families and individuals cared about the common good of all.

Our earth is God's planet—God's land. We don't own any part of it; neither does Israel. We are only stewards of the land we're on. God wants us to care for the earth and our environment. If we don't, and the land is destroyed or human beings made in God's image are destroyed or oppressed, we will suffer the consequences and so will our offspring. With global warming upon us—confirmed by 99 percent of climatologists and researchers—and plastics choking our oceans and toxic trash destroying our land masses, Christians need to pay attention if we care about future generations. And how much time do we leave for building real relationships with each other and with God, addicted as we are to our sports, our mobile devices, social media, and the internet? These are some of the challenges that lie ahead.

We will need to stop demonizing the other and learn how to listen to each other—especially those with different lifestyles and beliefs—and to work together to humbly bring this nation together again. Listening to each other while listening to God in silence and worship will be necessary. Some of us will be called to prayer and contemplation. Others will be called to prophetic speech, action, and advocacy.

When asked by one of my sisters in Christ what he thought was needed for those committed to prayer, fasting, and contemplation, Stephen Weaver responded by email that he would call Christians to a time of repentance and humility in these three areas:

1. Too much love of money
2. Indifference to the priorities of citizenship in God's domain
3. Giving in to political ideologies[5]

Here are some words of advice I adapted from the famous words of Martin Niemöller:[6]

> First, they came for the immigrants and refugees and I spoke up
> because immigrants and refugees are our neighbors.
> Then they came for black and brown people and I spoke up
> because black and brown people are our neighbors.

5. Weaver, emails to author.
6. See Holocaust Encyclopedia, "Martin Niemöller."

Then they came for the poor and the vulnerable and I spoke up
because the poor and vulnerable are our neighbors.
Then they came for the aid workers, the federal workers, and the civil servants and I spoke up
because they too are our neighbors.
Then they came for us, and we spoke up because we are all in this together and we are called to love all our neighbors, no exceptions.

Together we can be . . .

Turning the World's Values

Upside down!

ATTENTION CHURCH LEADERS

In 1954, Congress passed the Johnson amendment stating that if faith bodies that have tax exempt status endorse political candidates for office, they may lose their tax-exempt status. Since then, only one or two churches have had to do so after being taken to court. However, on July 7, 2025, a Texas district court judge ruled that when a house of worship "in good faith speaks to its congregation, through its customary channels of communication on matters of faith in connection with religious services, concerning electoral politics viewed through the lens of religious faith,"[7] it is

7. Quoted in Burke et al., "IRS Says," para. 6. See also Klimon et al., "IRS Enters into Consent."

not subject to the Johnson amendment, since that constitutes just a church discussion. Now the IRS has agreed with this ruling. We're dangerously moving closer to entwinement of church and state in the United States of America.

Here are some prophetic stances church leaders can take to make a difference:

- Join a multi-faith coalition, such as the gathering of clergy on Mondays at noon, called Moral Mondays, to protest and pray at the Capitol Building in Washington, DC.
- Write letters, call, or visit your senators and representatives.
- Be present at citizen rallies against ICE detention facilities and arrests. If you have a refugee resettlement agency in your community, ask what your church can do to help resettle refugees. If your church supports refugees, advise them to carry their papers with them wherever they go, and encourage your church to provide a place of safety for them.
- Defend health care and food and medicine aid for the poor around the world.
- Join Braver Angels and/or organize a series of respectful dialogues for faith community congregations on current church and state issues. See examples of respectful dialogue in the appendix following.
- Join the Church at a Crossroads movement to support Palestinian Christians.
- Remember to say the creeds and this prayer that Jesus taught:

Our Father in heaven
hallowed be your name,
your kingdom come,
your will be done,
on earth as in Heaven.
Give us today our daily bread.
Forgive us our sins,
as we forgive those who sin against us.
Save us from the time of trial,

and deliver us from evil.
For yours are the kingdom, the power, and the glory,
now and forever. Amen.[8]

8. Hill Country United Methodist Church, "Lord's Prayer."

Appendix

PRACTICING RESPECTFUL DIALOGUE

Dialogue Rules

CLASS OR GROUP WILL divide into groups of three. One person in each group will be an observer. The other two will dialogue.

- Each person in the dialogue will take turns stating his/her position on the question.
- The person speaking will use I statements.
- The person listening will paraphrase what the other person has said. Then, if the person speaking agrees that the paraphrase reflects what they have said, they will ask permission to share their rationale for holding that position, which may or may not include personal perspectives.
- The person listening may also ask the second person to say more about their position or ask questions.
- While the dialogue is taking place, the observer will stop any attempt of either speaker to demonize the other and make sure the guidelines are being followed. At the end of the conversation, the observer will ask the two participants to seek some common ground.

Dialogue One

Question: As a Christian in America, how do you describe yourself as a follower of Jesus?

Speaker 1: I became a follower of Jesus when I listened to Billy Graham telling the TV audience that Jesus was crucified just for me and that if I said the sinner's prayer, I would be saved. So, I did. He also encouraged all of us who said the prayer to join a church. So, I did. Then I was immersed to be baptized. Now that I am married and have a family, we joined a church, but sometimes we attend remotely because of sickness or conflicts in our busy schedules. My husband and I both work. Sundays are the only days we have just to relax, or our kids have sports contests we need to be present for. But we do attend worship services on special holidays as a family—like Christmas and Easter and special musical events. We also pledge to the church whatever we can afford. Since buying food for our growing family and fuel for our two cars costs more, we had to cut back on our pledge this year.

Speaker 2: (Responds by paraphrasing)

Speaker 2: In addition to being baptized and giving my life to Christ, I try to follow Jesus' teachings in my everyday life. Since Jesus ate and consorted with people from all circumstances, especially the poor and the outcast, I started helping feed the homeless at our local church, have taken into my home immigrants or refugees, and supported our local mission projects. I even had a chance to go on a mission trip—that trip was life changing. Jesus said that if I follow him, I can do even greater things than he did even though I fall short most of the time. He was God and we are only flawed human beings.

Speaker 1: (Responds by paraphrasing)

Dialogue continues . . .

(After 10–15 minutes of dialogue) *Observer*: Now that you have listened to and heard each other, tell me what you think you can both agree on.

Dialogue Two

Question: Do you believe the United States should be a Christian nation?

Speaker 1: This nation was founded by pilgrims who were Puritan separatists who first fled to Holland and who sought freedom from the hierarchy posed by the Church of England as well as economic opportunities in a new land. After the colonists won their freedom from England, they passed the first amendment to the Constitution giving us citizens these freedoms: to worship, to speak, to write or orally report, and to peacefully protest. In both England and Russia, church and state are intertwined. But in the United States, they are separate.

Speaker 2: (Responds by paraphrasing)

Speaker 2: The pilgrims—or Puritans as they were called—sought to establish a model Christian community and convert the Native Americans. That was the original intent of the founders of the United States and, as modern-day Christians, we need to restore what the pilgrims originally intended for America, starting with our institutions. The pilgrims put God first, and we need all our institutions to get away from wokeism and hypocrisy and make America once again a nation under God seeking to fulfill only his purposes, starting with a National Day of Repentance. America is the nation now chosen by God to prepare for Jesus' return, so let's make Jesus our commander-in-chief.

Speaker 1: (Responds by paraphrasing)

Dialogue continues . . .

(After 10–15 minutes of dialogue) *Observer*: Now that you have listened to and heard each other, tell me what you think you can both agree on.

Dialogue Three

Question: How does your Christian faith inform who you vote for?

Speaker 1: As a follower of Jesus, I know that Jesus was crucified for me. Our present president was chosen by God to lead this nation after being persecuted and almost martyred. He puts up with it because he is doing it for me. The Biden Justice Department and the FBI were out to get him in any way they can, even for taking presidential papers he wanted for his legacy. Poor man. He really takes care of those who are loyal to him. Besides, when he was president before, this country was on its way to being great again. He restored the federal courts with judges who rule by the Constitution, rebuilt our military, and was a peace maker in Israel and now in the Ukraine/Russian War. He chose Christian men and women to serve on his cabinet.

Speaker 2: (Responds by paraphrasing)

Speaker 2: Because of my Christian faith, I judge a candidate's fitness for an elected office by their experience and fitness to hold that office. Since our president is considered a leader of the free world, I look for whether they have experience and are respected by leaders in other countries. Above all, I try to assess the integrity and practice of their religious beliefs and whether they exhibit the qualities of integrity, humility, and honesty.

Speaker 1: (Responds by paraphrasing)

The dialogue continues . . .

(After 10–15 minutes of dialogue) *Observer*: Now that you have listened to and heard each other, tell me what you think you can both agree on.

Dialogue Four

Question: What should we Christians do about those seeking asylum in America?

Speaker 1: The majority of those seeking asylum at our southern border do so out of desperation and are escaping from threats of drug lords, drought, floods, gender-based violence, and religious persecution. I believe in the words on our Statue of Liberty. That lady has welcomed many of our ancestors who sought asylum and refuge in America. Besides, I believe that God cares about all humans, no matter what race or nationality they might be. In Matthew 25 and Luke 11, Jesus asks his followers to welcome strangers and offer them hospitality when they knock on our doors to ask for refuge.

Speaker 2: (Responds by paraphrasing)

Speaker 2: In biblical times, there were not the number of people we have now living on our planet. Too many are coming across our southern border. We need to complete the wall and send the hordes back to where they came from. Our current open border policy allows terrorists and criminals of all stripes to enter the country at will, aided and abetted by sanctuary cities. Anyone seeking asylum needs to come in legally and obey our laws or suffer the consequences. We should be stricter about those we let into the United States because the bad ones will even use children to bring in drugs. Now we have too many illegal immigrants taking advantage of all our social programs and public schools. We should only accept refugees who have skills that can advance our commerce. Just look at those trying to get permits to work in New York City and Chicago with all those immigrants crowding our cities! We can't even find housing for them!

Speaker 1: (Responds by paraphrasing)

The dialogue continues . . .

(After 10–15 minutes of dialogue) *Observer*: Now that you have listened to and heard each other, tell me what you think you can both agree on.

Author Notes

About the author's Christian heritage: Her father, grandfather, and great grandfather were pastors, so she was baptized and raised in church circles and among clergy. She graduated from Trinity School for Ministry, which became an Anglican seminary, thinking to follow in their footsteps, but God had other plans. The evolution of his plans she shares in her books *Who's Calling* and *Memories and Miracles*.

When Bishop Williams, a Hebrew biblical scholar, died, he was eulogized as a prophet of peace and justice. During his lifetime he preached and wrote about justice for the union workers in the automobile plant close to his home in Detroit. Henry Ford, then on his diocesan council, didn't like his preaching and told him so. Bishop Williams wrote a letter of resignation, but the other diocesan council members refused to let him go.

When the jovial bishop gathered his large family together for evening prayer every day he spoke lovingly about Jesus, his life and teachings, as well as the responsibilities of following Jesus during the height of the robber barons, the Mellons, the Fords, and the Rockefellers, who made billions at the expense of poor laborers.

The author's father, Benedict Williams, followed in his father's footsteps and became a parish pastor. The last parish he served was in a community where many CEOs of large corporations lived and worshiped in his church. His family benefited from their largesse—with hand-me-down clothes and even special trips on their private airplanes on occasion.

Dr. Webb, while grounded in the Protestant Episcopal tradition, has had a varied background worshiping in different denominational churches. During her spiritual journey, she has worshiped and retreated with Orthodox Christians, Roman Catholics, Lutherans, Mennonites, and nondenominational Christians. With that diverse background, she has grown to appreciate each tradition, as well as different ways to worship Jesus in this rich collage of Christ's Body while *being in the world and yet not of this world.* Currently, she sings in the choir at a United Methodist Church. Prior to that she was an active member of a local Mennonite church that had outgrown the building their forefathers built as many new families had joined. Some members are foster parents for African American children.

As a peacemaker, she was actively involved against the nuclear weapons buildup at the height of the Cold War. She started Peace Links in Pennsylvania with Teresa Heinz Kerry, served on her diocesan Peace Commission, and became an advocate for conflict resolution. She started recycling in Pennsylvania and was a chairperson for the first Earth Day. Along with William White, she founded Conservation Consultants. She has spent twenty years as a companion with the Community of Celebration, whose members spiritually grounded her citizenship as a missionary leader with Global Outreach for Addiction Leadership, or the GOAL Project.

Although retired, she became a published author. She says, "One never retires following where our Lord calls."

Website: https://marytheresawebb.com
LinkedIn: mary-theresa-webb
Email: authorterrywebb@gmail.com
Twitter: TrustingTerry
Facebook: Terry Webb
Substack: TrustTerry

Bibliography

Akin, Jimmy. "Who Was St. Francis of Assisi? 12 Things to Know and Share." *National Catholic Register*, Oct. 4, 2013. https://www.ncregister.com/blog/who-was-st-francis-of-assisi-12-things-to-know-and-share/.

Altman, Walter. "Interpreting the Doctrine of the Two Kingdoms: God's Kingship in the Church and in Politics." *Word & World*, July 1, 1987.

Aptowicz, Cristin O'Keefe. "Could You Stomach the Horrors of 'Halftime' in Ancient Rome?" Live Science, July 21, 2022. https://www.livescience.com/53615-horrors-of-the-colosseum.html.

Bethge, Eberhard. *Dietrich Bonhoeffer: A Biography*. Minneapolis: Fortress, 2000.

Biography.com. "Mother Teresa Biography." Last updated Feb. 24, 2020. www.biography.com/religious-figures/mother-teresa.

Boedy, Matthew. *The Seven Mountains Mandate: Exposing the Dangerous Plan to Christianize America and Destroy Democracy*. Louisville: Westminster John Knox, 2025.

Bonhoeffer, Dietrich. *The Cost of Discipleship*. New York: Macmillan, 1961.

———. *Dietrich Bonhoeffer: London, 1933–1935*. Vol. 13 of *Dietrich Bonhoeffer Works*. Edited by Keith W. Clements. Translated by Isabel Best. Minneapolis: Fortress, 2007.

Bowman, Hannah. "What the IRS's New Rules Mean for Churches." *Sojourners*, July 17, 2025. https://sojo.net/articles/opinion/what-irss-new-rules-mean-churches-speaking-out/.

Brown, Patrick T. "Man Does Not Live by Economic Growth Alone." *Public Discourse*, Dec. 3, 2018. https://www.thepublicdiscourse.com/2018/12/47392/.

Bunyan, John. *The Pilgrim's Progress*. Edited by Jesse Lyman Hurlbut. AmazonClassics, 2019. Kindle.

Burke, Daniel, et al. "IRS Says Churches Can Now Endorse Political Candidates." *Morning Edition*, July 8, 2025. NPR. https://www.npr.org/2025/07/08/nx-s1-5460886/irs-now-says-pastors-can-endorse-political-candidates.

Burton, Tara Isabella. "The Bible Says to Welcome Immigrants, So Why Don't Evangelicals?" Vox, Oct. 30, 2018. https://www.vox.com/2018/10/30/18035336/.

Byrd, Don. "New Poll: 29% of Americans Espouse Christian Nationalism, Unchanged from 2023." BJC, Feb. 14, 2025. https://bjconline.org/new-poll-29-of-americans-christian-nationalism-unchanged-from-2023-021425/.

Christians Against Christian Nationalism. "What Is Christian Nationalism?" Church and Community Resources. https://www.christiansagainstchristiannationalism.org/church-community-resources.

Claiborne, Shane, and Chris Haw. *Jesus for President: Politics for Ordinary Radicals*. Grand Rapids: Zondervan, 2008.

Cohen, Hagar, and Jacquelin Bouf. "Antisemitism Report Shows Marked Increase in Incidents and Neo-Nazi Activity." ABC News, Nov. 26, 2018. https://www.abc.net.au/news/2018-11-26/antisemitism-report-shows-marked-increase-in-incidents-australia/10555264.

Connolly, Peter. *The Jews in the Time of Jesus: A History*. Oxford: Oxford University Press, 1994.

Constitution of the United States of America. National Constitution Center. https://constitutioncenter.org/the-constitution.

Davis, F. Reginald. *We Need Each Other to Transform America*. Mechanicsburg, PA: Scriptoria, 2025.

Dewey, Donald. "Madison's Views on Electoral Reform." *Western Political Quarterly* 15.1 (1962) 140–45.

"Dietrich Bonhoeffer: Theologian in Nazi Germany." Special issue, *Christian History* 32 (1991). https://www.christianitytoday.com/christian-history/1991/issue-32/.

Dreher, Rod. *The Benedict Option: A Strategy for Christians in a Post-Christian Nation*." New York: Penguin, 2017.

Egan, Eileen, and Kathleen Egan. *Blessed Are You, Mother Teresa and the Beatitudes*. Ann Arbor, MI: Servant, 1992.

Eisenhower, Dwight. "Quotes," Dwight D. Eisenhower Presidential Library, Museum and Boyhood Home (website). https://www.eisenhowerlibrary.gov/eisenhowers/quotes/.

Encyclopaedia Britannica. "Israeli-Palestinian Conflict Explained." https://www.britannica.com/explore/israeli-palestinian-conflicts.

———. "Mother Teresa." https://www.britannica.com/biography/Mother-Teresa.

———. "St. Francis of Assisi." https://www.britannica.com/biography/Saint-Francis-of-Assisi.

The Episcopal Church. *The Book of Common Prayer*. New York: Oxford University Press, 1990.

Eylon, Lili. "Anti-Semitism: The Controversy over Richard Wagner." Jewish Virtual Library. https://www.jewishvirtuallibrary.org/richard-wagner-controversy.

Facing History and Ourselves. "Protestant Churches and the Nazi State." Last updated Aug. 2, 2016. https://www.facinghistory.org/holocaust-and-human-behavior/chapter-5/protestant-churches-and-nazi-state/.

Forest, Jim. *The Ladder of the Beatitudes*. Maryknoll, NY: Orbis, 1999.

Frum, David. *Trumpocracy: The Corruption of the American Republic.* New York: HarperCollins, 2018.

Gaines-Cirelli, Ginger. *Sacred Resistance: A Practical Guide to Christian Witness and Dissent.* Nashville: Abingdon, 2018.

Gibbon, Edward. *The Decline and Fall of the Roman Empire.* New York: Modern Library, 2003.

Granberg-Michaelson, Wesley. "When Seminary Becomes a Threat." *Sojourners,* Feb. 2018. https://sojo.net/magazine/february-2018/when-seminary-becomes-threat.

Hale, Lori Brandt, and Reggie L. Williams. "Is This a Bonhoeffer Moment?" *Sojourners,* Feb. 2018. https://sojo.net/magazine/february-2018/bonhoeffer-moment.

Hill, Kent. *The Puzzle of the Soviet Church: An Inside Look at Christianity and Glasnost.* Portland: Multnomah, 1989.

Hill, Wesley. "The Strange New World of the Beatitudes." *Comment,* Sept. 21, 2017. https://comment.org/the-strange-new-world-of-the-beatitudes.

Hill Country United Methodist Church. "The Lord's Prayer (Ecumenical Version)." https://hillcountryumc.org/lords-prayer/.

Hillerbrand, Hans J. "Martin Luther." https://www.britannica.com/biography/Martin-Luther.

History.com. "Ancient Rome." https://www.history.com/topics/ancient-rome.

Holocaust Encyclopedia. "Martin Niemöller: 'First They Came For . . .'" United States Holocaust Memorial Museum (website), last updated Apr. 11, 2023. https://encyclopedia.ushmm.org/content/en/article/martin-niemoeller-first-they-came-for-the-socialists.

Horton, Michael. "What Are Evangelicals Afraid of Losing?" *Christianity Today,* Aug. 31, 2018. https://www.christianitytoday.com/2018/08/evangelicals-trump-elections-losing-everything/.

Jefferson, Thomas. "Letter to the Danbury Baptists." Jan. 1, 1802. https://www.loc.gov/loc/lcib/9806/danpre.html.

Jeremiah, David. *The Great Disappearance: 31 Ways to Be Rapture Ready.* Nashville: Thomas Nelson, 2023.

Jones, Robert P. "The Roots of Christian Nationalism Go Back Further Than You Think." *Time,* Aug. 31, 2023. https://time.com/6309657/us-christian-nationalism-columbus-essay/.

Kalisha, Grace. "A Problem Well-Defined Is a Problem Half-Solved." LinkedIn, Aug. 13, 2019. https://www.linkedin.com/pulse/problem-well-defined-half-solved-grace-kalisha.

Kaufman, Jack, dir. *The Rise and Fall of the Third Reich.* 1968. Burbank, CA: Warner Archive, 2012.

Kelkar, Kamala. "Electoral College Is 'Vestige' of Slavery, Say Some Constitutional Scholars." PBS NewsHour, Nov. 6, 2016. https://www.pbs.org/newshour/politics/electoral-college-slavery-constitution.

Klimon, William M., et al. "The IRS Enters into Consent Decree Limiting Application of Johnson Amendment; New Position Allows Churches to Endorse Candidates in Certain Situations." *National Law Review*, Jul. 14, 2025. https://natlawreview.com/article/irs-enters-consent-decree-limiting-application-johnson-amendment-new-position.

Knapp, Wilfrid F., et al. "Adolf Hitler." https://www.britannica.com/biography/Adolf-Hitler.

Kraybill, Donald B. *The Upside-Down Kingdom*. Scottdale, PA: Herald, 1978.

Larson, Erik. *In the Garden of the Beasts: Love, Terror, and an American Family in Hitler's Berlin*. New York: Crown, 2011. Kindle.

Martinez, Jessica, and Smith, Gregory A. "How the Faithful Voted: A Preliminary 2016 Analysis." Pew Research Center, Nov. 9, 2016. https://www.pewresearch.org/short-reads/2016/11/09/how-the-faithful-voted-a-preliminary-2016-analysis/.

Matthews, J. F., et al. "Constantine I." https://www.britannica.com/biography/Constantine-I-Roman-emperor.

McCrummen, Stephanie. "The Army of God." *Atlantic*, Jan. 9, 2025. https://www.theatlantic.com/magazine/archive/2025/02/new-apostolic-reformation-christian-movement-trump/681092/.

Melton, J. Gordon, et al. "Christian Fundamentalism." https://www.britannica.com/topic/Christian-fundamentalism.

Miller, Paul D. "People Are Still Confused About Christian Nationalism." *Christianity Today*, Mar. 3, 2023. https://www.christianitytoday.com/2023/03/christian-nationalism-ct-white-evangelical-america-religion/.

Moore, Russell. "The Church Better Start Taking Nazification Seriously," *Christianity Today*, Nov. 5, 2025. https://www.christianitytoday.com/2025/11/nazism-nick-fuentes-tucker-carlson/.

Niebuhr, H. Richard. *Christ and Culture*. San Francisco: Harper, 1951.

Novo, Andrew R. "Ukraine and the Lessons of Munich." *Europe's Edge*, Feb. 10, 2025. CEPA. https://cepa.org/article/ukraine-and-the-lessons-of-munich/.

Orthodox Wiki. "Fool-for-Christ." https://orthodoxwiki.org/Fool-for-Christ.

PBS News. "Rev. Russell Levenson Jr. Delivers Homily at Funeral for George H. W. Bush." PBS NewsHour, Dec. 5, 2018. YouTube video, 12:42. https://www.youtube.com/watch?v=ms6hvvaop80.

Perkins, Pheme. *Hearing the Parables of Jesus*. New York: Paulist, 1981.

Pew Research Center. "U.S. Protestants in Evangelical and Historically Black Traditions Especially Likely to Believe Humanity Is 'Living in the End Times.'" Washington, DC. Dec. 7, 2022. https://www.pewresearch.org/short-reads/2022/12/08/about-four-in-ten-u-s-adults-believe-humanity-is-living-in-the-end-times/ft_22-12-08_endtimes_01-png/.

Philip, Aaron. "The New Prophecy: Echoes of Montanism in the New Apostolic Reformation." *Modern Reformation*, May 2, 2024. https://www.modernreformation.org/resources/essays/the-new-prophecy-echoes-of-montanism-in-the-new-apostolic-reformation.

Rodgers, John. *Essential Truths for Christians.* Blue Bell, PA: Classical Anglican, 2011.

Rodney, Aaron. "Constantine's Vision: The Turning Point for Christianity." *History in 5* (blog), Mar. 24, 2025. https://history-in-5.com/2025/03/24/constantines-vision-the-turning-point-for-christianity/.

Rosen, Jeffrey, and David Rubenstein. "The Declaration, the Constitution, and the Bill of Rights." National Constitution Center. https://constitutioncenter.org/the-constitution/white-papers/the-declaration-the-constitution-and-the-bill-of-rights.

Ruth, Janet. *One Nation Under God.* Enumclaw, WA: Redemption, 2005.

Ryan, Missy. "Holy Warrior." *Atlantic*, Oct. 22, 2025. https://www.theatlantic.com/national-security/archive/2025/10/pete-hegseth-christianity-pentagon/684645/.

Saiya, Nilay. "The Varieties of American Christian Nationalism." *Politics and Religion* 18 (2025) 171–89. doi:10.1017/S1755048325000069.

Seinfeldism.com. "S06E16—The Beard." https://seinfeldism.com/s06e16-the-beard.php.

Sider, Ron. "God's People Reconciling." 1984. CPT. https://cpt.org/sider.

Siegele-Wenschkewitz, Leonore. "Christians Against Nazis: The German Confessing Church." *Christian History* 9 (1986). https://www.christianitytoday.com/1986/01/christians-against-nazis-german-confessing-church/.

SPLC. "Leaked Emails Expose Key White House Aide Stephen Miller's Affinity for White Nationalism. SPLC Press Center, Nov. 12, 2019. https://www.splcenter.org/presscenter/splc-leaked-emails-expose-key-white-house-aide-stephen-millers-affinity-white/.

St. Matthews Episcopal Church. "How the Apostles Died." https://www.saginawstmatthews.org/how-the-apostles-died.

Strang, Stephen. *Trump Aftershock: The President's Seismic Impact on Culture and Faith in America.* Lake Mary, FL: Frontline, 2018.

Thomas à Kempis. *The Imitation of Christ.* Peabody, MA: Hendrickson, 2004.

Timeless Myths. "What Was Israel Before 1948? What Led to the Creation of Israel?" Last modified Mar. 8, 2024. https://timelessmyths.com/stories/what-was-israel-before-1948.

The United Methodist Hymnal: Book of United Methodist Worship. Nashville: United Methodist Publishing House, 1989.

Ushistory.org. "The Roman Republic." Ancient Civilizations Online Textbook. http://www.ushistory.org/civ/6a.asp.

Villegas, Isaac Samuel. *Migrant God. A Christian Vision of Immigrant Justice.* Grand Rapids: Eerdmans, 2025.

Webb, Mary Theresa. *Memories and Miracles.* CreateSpace, 2017.

Webb, Terry. "No Longer Underground." *Charisma*, Jan. 2000, 57–60.

———. *Tree of Renewed Life: Spiritual Renewal of the Church through the Twelve-Step Program.* New York: Crossroads, 1992.

Weber, Hans-Ruedi. *Salty Christians.* New York: Seabury, 1967.

Whitehead, Andrew L. *American Idolatry: How Christian Nationalism Betrays the Gospel and Threatens the Church*. Grand Rapids: Brazos, 2023.

———. "3 Threats Christian Nationalism Poses to the United States." *Time*, Sept. 26, 2022. https://time.com/6214724/christian-nationalism-threats-united-states/.

Whitehead, Andrew L., and Perry, Samuel L. *Taking America Back For God*. New York: Oxford University Press, 2020.

Wikipedia. "Adolf Hitler's Cult of Personality." https://en.wikipedia.org/wiki/Adolf_Hitler's_cult_of_personality.

———. "Date of the Birth of Jesus." https://en.wikipedia.org/wiki/Date_of_the_birth_of_Jesus.

———. "Dominion Theology." https://en.wikipedia.org/wiki/Dominion_theology.

———. "Francis of Assisi." https://en.wikipedia.org/wiki/Francis_of_Assisi.

———. "Herod the Great." https://en.wikipedia.org/wiki/Herod_the_Great.

———. "History of the Church of England." https://en.wikipedia.org/wiki/History_of_the_Church_of_England.

———. "Mother Teresa." https://en.wikipedia.org/wiki/Mother_Teresa.

———. "Prayer of St. Francis." https://en.wikipedia.org/wiki/prayer_of_Saint_Francis.

———. "Wars of the Three Kingdoms." https://en.wikipedia.org/wiki/Wars_of_the_Three_Kingdoms.

Wilkins, Brett. "Report Details 400+ Attacks on Science in First 6 Months of Trump 2.0." Common Dreams, July 21, 2025. https://www.commondreams.org/news/trump-attack-on-science.

Wright, N. T. *Simply Jesus: A New Vision of Who He Was, What He Did, and Why He Matters*. New York: HarperOne, 2011.

Young, Wm. Paul. *The Shack: Where Tragedy Confronts Eternity*. Newbury Park, CA: Windblown Media, 2007.

Zurlo, Gina. "World Christianity: It's Annual Statistical Table Time!" Overseas Ministries Study Center. Princeton Theological Seminary. 2025. https://omsc.ptsem.edu/world-christianity-its-annual-statistical-table-time/.

RECOMMENDED WEBSITES

Christians Against Christian Nationalism:
www.christiansagainstchristiannationalism.org

Friends Committee on National Legislation:
www.fcnl.org

Red Letter Christians:
www.redletterchristians.org

Vote Common Good:
www.votecommongood.com

www.ingramcontent.com/pod-product-compliance
Lightning Source LLC
LaVergne TN
LVHW050650100826
845148LV00011B/2054